Latin Momentum Tests for GCSE

LATIN
MOMENTUM TESTS
FOR GCSE

Ashley Carter

Bristol Classical Press

First published in 2003 by
Bristol Classical Press,
an imprint of
Bloomsbury Academic
Bloomsbury Publishing Plc
50 Bedford Square
London WC1B 3DP
&
175 Fifth Avenue,
New York, NY 10010, USA

A catalogue record for this book
is available from the British Library

ISBN 978-1-85-399667-2

Printed and bound by CPI Group (UK) Ltd, Croydon, CR0 4YY

www.bloomsburyacademic.com

Cover illustration: Aeneas' fleet. Engraving from Aeneid III,
edited by J. Zempel (Rome, 1763–5).

Contents

Contents

Introduction for the Teacher

This series of twenty momentum tests has been designed to provide students preparing to enter for GCSE Latin with appropriate practice materials. The first five tests are set at Foundation Tier standard, the remaining fifteen at Higher Tier standard. All the tests are modelled on those set by one of the examination boards, scheduled for first appearance in the summer of 2003.

The purpose of a momentum test is to test students' comprehension of and ability to translate a previously unseen Latin story. Comprehension is tested through the first and third sections of each story; the second section is for translation. There is a gradient of difficulty throughout each test, manifested by increasing complexity of the Latin and more demanding comprehension questions.

The stories have been selected to provide a balance of mythological and historical themes, with most being derived from poetry, a resource as yet untapped for use in examinations. In all cases the Latin has been completely reworked so as to generate a reasonable uniformity of style and difficulty (though some variation in both is inevitable), to make use as far as possible of the vocabulary knowledge expected of GCSE entrants, and to include as wide a range of syntactical structures as is appropriate at this level.

The book is designed for use directly by the student, with the needs both of those students without regular access to a qualified Latin teacher, and of the increasing number of teachers who are working under severe time pressures borne in mind. To these ends full mark schemes have been provided at the end of the book. The mark schemes for the comprehension sections follow exactly the pattern of those used in the public examinations; those for the translation sections, however, are presented differently, with the marks appearing over the English rather than the Latin version. This is to enable students themselves to mark their own translations. The principle of assigning two marks to most inflected words still applies, and the resulting final mark, if the scheme is applied carefully enough, should be as precise as if an examiner had marked the test.

Providing mark schemes does of course raise the possibility that students may 'cheat', i.e. look up the answers rather than work the Latin out for themselves. Teachers consulted during the preparation of this book were evenly divided over whether they thought their own students would be likely to cheat and, therefore, over the desirability of including such mark schemes. Teachers who may fear cheating do have the option, however, of setting part or all of each test as a classroom exercise, where they can ensure that no one turns to the back of the book. Conversely, those teachers who feel they can trust their students can set the tests as homework.

One advantage of including mark schemes is the clear benefit of student self-assessment. A student who carefully marks his or her own test will gain much more from the exercise than one who simply hands it to someone else to mark. Errors will

1

be noted and explained, vocabulary knowledge will be reinforced and syntactical structures will be worked through much more effectively when the feedback is immediate and self-instigated. Teachers will still have the opportunity to look through their students' work after they have marked it.

The author is grateful to Alan Clague for all the help and advice given by him during the planning and preparation of this book, and to the students of Hitchin Girls' School for piloting some of the tests.

A Note to the Student

Please remember as you do these tests that, in the actual examination, presentation and legibility are important. You are therefore advised to get into the habit now of writing your translation on alternate lines and leaving a blank line between each answer. When you come to mark your work, you will see the benefit of this.

Words which you are not expected to know will be glossed the first time they appear in each story. You should note that many words that are glossed in Section 1 of a story will recur in Sections 2 or 3, where they will *not* be glossed again. This is different from the practice in examination papers.

Foundation Tier Tests

I. MIDAS

1 Read the first section of the story carefully, then answer all the questions.

Midas celebrated when his people brought
Silenus to him.

1 Midas erat rex Phrygiae. olim pauci Phrygii senem ebrium in silvis
2 ceperunt. hic senex erat Silenus, qui amicus dei Bacchi erat. Phrygii senem
3 ad Midam duxerunt. ubi rex cognovit quis esset, laetus fuit. decem dies
   noctesque omnibus civibus epulas dedit; Silenus enim erat hospes illustris.
   honoribus ita datis, Midas senem Baccho reddidit.

Names

Midas, Midae (m)	Midas
Phrygia, Phrygiae (f)	Phrygia (a country in Asia)
Phrygii, Phrygiorum (m pl)	Phrygians, people of Phrygia
Silenus, Sileni (m)	Silenus
Bacchus, Bacchi (m)	Bacchus

Vocabulary

ebrius, ebria, ebrium	drunk
epulae, epularum (f pl)	feast, banquet
hospes, hospitis (m)	guest
illustris, illustre	honoured, famous
honor, honoris (m)	honour

(a)	Who was Midas?	[1]
(b)	*olim…ceperunt* (lines 1-2): explain how Silenus was captured.	[3]
(c)	*hic…erat* (line 2): what **two** things are we told about Silenus here?	[2]
(d)	What did the Phrygians do with Silenus?	[1]
(e)	*ubi…fuit* (line 3): explain how the king felt.	[3]
(f)	How did Midas celebrate the arrival of Silenus?	[3]
(g)	What did Midas do after the celebration?	[2]

[15]

7

2 Read this section carefully and then translate it into English. **Please write your translation on alternate lines.**

Midas was delighted to choose a reward from Bacchus.

amico reddito, deus promisit se donum Midae daturum esse. 'tibi dabo' inquit 'quidquid vis.' 'omnia quae tango in aurum verte' Midas deo respondit. quamquam deus tristis fuit quod Midas tam stultus erat, ei donum quod petiverat dedit.

rex abiit gaudens. ramum ab arbore abripuit: statim ramus aureus factus est. ubi ianuam domus suae tetigit, ianua quoque aurea fuit. etiam aqua in qua manum posuit aurea fuit. ita rex sperabat se mox divitissimum futurum esse.

Vocabulary

quidquid	whatever
tango, tangere, tetigi, tactus	I touch
aurum, auri (n)	gold
ramus, rami (m)	branch
arbor, arboris (f)	tree
aureus, aurea, aureum	made of gold
spero, sperare, speravi, speratus	I hope
dives, divitis	rich

[25]

I. *MIDAS*

3 Read this final section of the story carefully, then answer all the questions.

Midas regretted his choice of gift.

1 deinde servi cenam regi posuerunt. rex <u>panem</u> ad <u>os</u> tulit, sed <u>panis</u> <u>durus</u>
   fuit. vinum ex aureo <u>poculo</u> bibere voluit, sed cum vinum <u>os</u> tetigisset,
3 aureum factum est. iam Midas intellexit quam stultus fuisset. <u>bracchiis</u>
   <u>splendidis</u> ad caelum <u>sublatis</u>, deum <u>oravit</u> ut sibi <u>parceret</u>. Bacchus, quod
   <u>benignus</u> erat, regem servavit.

Based on Ovid, *Metamorphoses* XI.90-135.

Vocabulary

panis, panis (m)	bread
os, oris (n)	mouth
durus, dura, durum	hard
poculum, poculi (n)	cup
bracchium, bracchii (n)	arm
splendidus, splendida, splendidum	shining, gleaming
tollo, tollere, sustuli, sublatus	I raise
oro, orare, oravi, oratus	I beg
parco, parcere, peperci + dat.	I spare
benignus, benigna, benignum	kind

(a) In line 1, what did the king's slaves do?   [2]

(b) *rex…factum est* (lines 1-3): describe in detail the **two** difficulties
that the king experienced.   [3 + 6]

(c) *iam…fuisset* (line 3): what did Midas now realise?   [2]

(d) What did Midas do to try to restore his situation to normal?   [4]

(e) What response did he receive?   [3]

[20]

Total [60]

II. *PICUS AND CANENS*

1 Read the first section of the story carefully, then answer all the questions.

Picus loved only Canens, though many girls loved him.

1 <u>Picus</u> erat rex <u>Ausoniae</u>. tam pulcher erat rex ut multae puellae quae in
2 <u>Ausonia</u> habitabant eum amarent. cotidie <u>turba</u> puellarum ad domum eius
3 conveniebat ut eum spectarent. <u>Picus</u> tamen omnes puellas <u>spernebat</u> <u>nisi</u>
4 unam. haec puella non solum pulchrior omnibus aliis erat sed etiam
5 cantabat tam <u>suaviter</u> ut nomen '<u>Canens</u>' ei daretur. <u>Canens</u> <u>Picum</u> amabat.

Names

Picus, Pici (m)	Picus
Ausonia, Ausoniae (f)	Ausonia
Canens, Canentis (f)	Canens (lit. 'Songstress')

Vocabulary

turba, turbae (f)	crowd
sperno, spernere, sprevi, spretus	I reject
nisi	except
suaviter	sweetly

(a) Who was Picus?   [1]
(b) *tam...amarent* (lines 1-2):
    (i)   what was special about Picus?   [1]
    (ii) what happened as a result of this special feature?   [3]
(c) In lines 2-3, what happened every day?   [3]
(d) How did Picus react to this daily event?   [3]
(e) *haec puella...daretur* (lines 4-5):
    (i)   give the **two** special qualities that *haec puella* possessed.   [3]
    (ii) what happened as a result of the second of these qualities?   [1]

                                             [15]

II. *PICUS AND CANENS*

2 Read this section carefully and then translate it into English. **Please write your translation on alternate lines.**

The witch Circe trapped Picus.

olim Picus domo exiit ut <u>apros</u> in silvis peteret. <u>Circe</u>, quae <u>saga</u> dira erat, in eisdem silvis ambulabat. ubi Picum conspexit, eum cupiebat. quod equus Picum celeriter ab ea portabat, non statim eum capere <u>potuit</u>.

<u>aprum</u> igitur ingentem ad eum misit. Picus, cum <u>aprum</u> vidisset, eum capere et necare voluit. ab equo <u>desiluit</u> perque silvas festinavit. mox <u>procul</u> ab amicis fuit. subito <u>ante</u> eum stabat <u>Circe</u>, quae eum rogavit ut <u>amorem</u> suum acciperet et redderet.

Names

Circe, Circes (f)	Circe

Vocabulary

aper, apri (m)	(wild) boar
saga, sagae (f)	witch
possum, posse, potui	I am able
desilio, desilire, desilui	I jump down
procul	far away
ante + acc.	before
amor, amoris (m)	love

[25]

3   Read this final section of the story carefully, then answer all the questions.

Both Picus and Canens, now husband and wife, died.

1   sed Picus 'quisquis es' inquit 'ego non sum tuus; nam aliam amo et semper
2   amabo.' Circe irata fuit: 'poenas dabis' inquit 'si me ita spernes. numquam
    ad Canentem redibis.' quamquam Picus celerrime fugit, effugere non
    potuit. Canens, cum maritus domum non rediisset, multos dies eum
    quaerebat, sed frustra. tandem exspiravit.

Based on Ovid, Metamorphoses XIV.320-434.

Vocabulary

quisquis	whoever
poenas do, dare, dedi, datus	I am punished
maritus, mariti (m)	husband
exspiro, exspirare, exspiravi	I die

(a) In lines 1-2, what reply did Picus make to Circe?   [4]
(b) How did Circe react to Picus' words?   [6]
(c) Describe the last moments of Picus.   [4]
(d) When did Canens become anxious for her husband?   [2]
(e) What did Canens do to relieve her anxiety?   [2]
(f) Write down and translate the Latin word that tells you Canens was
         unsuccessful.   [2]

[20]

Total [60]

III. *DAEDALUS AND ICARUS*

1. Read the first section of the story carefully, then answer all the questions.

Daedalus devised a strange plan to enable him to leave Crete.

1 Daedalus erat artifex, qui multos annos in insula Creta habitabat. iam
2 Athenas redire volebat, ubi natus erat. rex tamen Cretae eum iussit in Creta
3 manere. 'rex' inquit Daedalus 'quamquam terram et mare regit, caelum non
4 tenet.' his verbis dictis, Daedalus alas facere coepit. in terra multas pennas
   et breves et longas posuit. has cera colligavit.

Names

Daedalus, Daedali (m)	Daedalus
Creta, Cretae (f)	Crete
Athenae, Athenarum (f pl)	Athens

Vocabulary

artifex, artificis (m)	craftsman
natus, nata, natum	born
rego, regere, rexi, rectus	I rule, control
ala, alae (f)	wing
coepi, coepisse	I began
penna, pennae (f)	feather
brevis, breve	short
cera, cerae (f)	wax
colligo, colligare, colligavi, colligatus	I bind together

(a)	What are we told about Daedalus in line 1?	[4]
(b)	*iam…erat* (lines 1-2): what did Daedalus want to do, and why?	[2]
(c)	What prevented Daedalus from doing what he wanted?	[2]
(d)	*rex…tenet* (lines 3-4): what contrast does Daedalus make here?	[4]
(e)	Describe in detail the making of the wings.	[3]

[15]

2   Read this section carefully and then translate it into English. **Please write your translation on alternate lines.**

Daedalus made wings for himself and his young son, Icarus.

Daedalus alas sibi <u>confecit</u>; alae optimae erant. ubi alae paratae erant, artifex se in caelum iecit, corpus alis <u>tollens</u>. cum intellexisset alas se facile portare, alteras alas filio suo, <u>Icaro</u> nomine, fecit. noluit enim <u>sine</u> filio effugere.

his quoque <u>confectis</u>, puerum monuit ut <u>cursum</u> medium teneret: 'si prope mare <u>volabis</u>' inquit 'undae alas graves facient, et in mare <u>decides</u>; si tamen prope <u>solem</u> <u>volabis</u>, <u>calor</u> pennas incendet. si prope me <u>volabis</u>, nullum periculum tibi erit.'

Names

Icarus, Icari (m)   Icarus

Vocabulary

conficio, conficere, confeci, confectus	I complete
tollo, tollere, sustuli, sublatus	I lift up
sine + abl.	without
cursus, cursus (m)	course
volo, volare, volavi	I fly
decido, decidere, decidi	I fall down
sol, solis (m)	sun
calor, caloris (m)	heat

[25]

III. *DAEDALUS AND ICARUS*

3 Read this final section of the story carefully, then answer all the questions.

Icarus disobeyed his father's instructions and died.

1 deinde et pater et filius se in caelum sustulerunt. multas horas iter laeti
2 fecerunt. tum puer, novis alis <u>delectatus</u>, altius volare <u>coepit</u>. cum sol
   ceram <u>mollem</u> fecisset, omnes pennae in mare deciderunt; decidit Icarus
4 quoque. ubi pater respexit, filium non vidit. eum late quaerens, tandem
   pennas inter undas vidit. corpus receptum in <u>sepulcro</u> tristis posuit.

Based on Ovid, Metamorphoses VIII.183-235.

Vocabulary

delectatus, delectata, delectatum	delighted
coepi, coepisse	I began
mollis, molle	soft
sepulcrum, sepulcri (n)	tomb

(a) *deinde…sustulerunt* (line 1): what happened then? [3]
(b) How long were they *laeti*? [1]
(c) *tum…coepit* (line 2): what did the boy then do, and why? [4]
(d) What happened to the boy's wings? [4]
(e) In lines 2-4, what happened to Icarus? [1]
(f) *ubi…vidit* (line 4):
    (i) when did Daedalus notice that his son was not in sight? [1]
    (ii) explain how Daedalus finally learned what had happened to Icarus. [4]
(g) What happened to Icarus' body? [2]

[20]

Total [60]

IV. CEPHALUS AND PROCRIS

1 Read the first section of the story carefully, then answer all the questions.

Cephalus visited some friends and began to tell the story of the strange spear he was carrying.

1 <u>Cephalus</u> erat senex. ad insulam <u>Aeginam</u> venit. hic amicos habebat, quos
2 multos annos non viderat. unus ex amicis eum rogavit de <u>hasta</u> quam
3 portabat. <u>Cephalus</u> respondit <u>hastam</u> <u>mirabilem</u> esse; 'sed semper lacrimo'
4 inquit 'ubi hanc <u>hastam</u> specto. nam mortem meae <u>uxori</u> tulit. <u>uxor</u> erat
5 <u>Procris</u>, femina pulcherrima et <u>suavissima</u>, quam ego maxime amabam.'

Names

Cephalus, Cephali (m)	Cephalus
Aegina, Aeginae (f)	Aegina
Procris (*acc. Procrin*)	Procris

Vocabulary

hasta, hastae (f)	spear
mirabilis, mirabile	strange, wonderful
uxor, uxoris (f)	wife
suavis, suave	sweet

(a) *Cephalus erat senex* (line 1): what information are we given about Cephalus? [1]

(b) In line 1, what sort of place did Cephalus travel to? [1]

(c) In lines 1-2, what are we told about Cephalus' friends? [2]

(d) In lines 2-3, what enquiry did the friend make? [2]

(e) *Cephalus…esse* (line 3): what was Cephalus' reply here? [1]

(f) *sed…tulit* (lines 3-4):
    (i) what did Cephalus say had happened when he looked at the spear? [2]
    (ii) What reason did Cephalus give for this? [2]

(g) From line 5, give **four** details about Cephalus' wife. [4]

[15]

IV. *CEPHALUS AND PROCRIS*

2   Read this section carefully and then translate it into English. **Please write your translation on alternate lines.**

Cephalus describes how Aurora ruined his marriage to Procris.

Cephalus fabulam de vita sua amicis narrabat. 'olim' inquit 'dea <u>Aurora</u> me conspexit et abstulit, quod me amavit. sed ego eam amare nolui, quod uxorem <u>malebam</u>. irata me uxori tandem reddidit; sed promisit nos miseros futuros esse.

<u>dum</u> domum ambulo, timere <u>coepi</u>: Procrisne etiam tum fidelis erat? <u>Aurora</u> <u>speciem</u> meam <u>mutavit</u>, ut Procrin spectarem <u>clam</u>que <u>tentarem</u>. Procris, quae me non cognoverat, primum meum <u>amorem</u> accipere nolebat; sed tandem <u>haesitavit</u>. statim eam <u>damnavi</u>.'

Names

Aurora, Aurorae (f)   Aurora (goddess of the dawn)

Vocabulary

malo, malle, malui	I prefer
dum	while
coepi, coepisse	I began
species, speciei (f)	appearance
muto, mutare, mutavi, mutatus	I disguise, change
clam	secretly
tento, tentare, tentavi, tentatus	I test
amor, amoris (m)	love
haesito, haesitare, haesitavi, haesitatus	I hesitate
damno, damnare, damnavi, damnatus	I condemn

[25]

3 Read this final section of the story carefully, then answer all the questions.

Cephalus accidentally killed his wife with the spear.

1 Cephalus 'statim' inquit 'Procris e domo in montes fugit, ubi deam <u>Dianam</u>
2 <u>coluit</u>. ego tamen eam inventam <u>oravi</u> ut mihi <u>ignosceret</u>. itaque domum
3 mecum rediit, et multos annos laetissimi eramus. olim hanc hastam, quam
4 dea ei dederat, ad <u>venationem</u> portavi. nescivi Procrin post me ire. ubi
aliquid <u>moveri</u> conspexi, hastam <u>emisi</u>; hasta Procrin necavit.'

Based on Ovid, Metamorphoses VII.661-865.

Names

Diana, Dianae (f)   Diana

Vocabulary

colo, colere, colui, cultus	I worship
oro, orare, oravi, oratus	I beg
ignosco, ignoscere, ignovi, ignotus + dat.	I forgive
venatio, venationis (f)	hunt, hunting
moveo, movere, movi, motus	I move
emitto, emittere, emisi, emissus	I throw

(a) *Cephalus…coluit* (lines 1-2): what, according to Cephalus, did Procris do?   [4]
(b) In line 2, what did Cephalus do in response to these actions of Procris?   [3]
(c) In lines 2-3, what **two** events prove that Procris forgave Cephalus?   [4]
(d) **(i)**   In line 4, why did Cephalus take Procris' spear?   [1]
       (ii)   How had Procris obtained this spear?   [2]
(e) *nescivi…ire* (line 4): what did Cephalus not know?   [2]
(f) Explain how and why Procris died.   [4]

[20]

Total [60]

V. *NERO AND AGRIPPINA*

1 Read the first section of the story carefully, then answer all the questions.

The Emperor Nero decided to kill his mother.

1 Nero Poppaeam maxime amabat. Agrippina, mater Neronis, Poppaeam
2 oderat. Nero igitur matrem suam necare constituit. amicos rogavit quo
3 modo eam necare posset. placuit primo venenum, sed difficile erat
  venenum ei nescienti dare. tandem Anicetus libertus consilium optimum
5 cepit. 'navem aedificare possum' inquit. 'ubi Agrippina in hac nave
  navigabit, tectum navis in eam decidet. in hoc modo necabitur.'

Names

Nero, Neronis (m)	Nero
Poppaea, Poppaeae (f)	Poppaea
Agrippina, Agrippinae (f)	Agrippina
Anicetus, Aniceti (m)	Anicetus

Vocabulary

odi, odisse	I hate
possum, posse, potui	I am able, I can
placet, placere, placuit + dat	it pleases
venenum, veneni (n)	poison
tectum, tecti (n)	(here) cabin roof
decido, decidere, decidi	I fall down

(a) In lines 1-2, what was the relationship between
   (i) Nero and Poppaea? [2]
   (ii) Agrippina and Poppaea? [1]
(b) In line 2, what did Nero decide to do? [1]
(c) What did Nero ask his friends? [2]
(d) *venenum* (line 3):
   (i) what was Nero's attitude to this suggestion at first? [1]
   (ii) why did he then reject this suggestion? [3]
(e) Suggest a suitable translation in this context for *cepit* (line 5). [1]
(f) Describe in detail Anicetus' plan. [4]

[15]

2 Read this section carefully and then translate it into English. **Please write your translation on alternate lines.**

> *Anicetus' plan was put into action, but it did not work as intended.*

Anicetus Neroni persuadebat ut navis aedificaretur. 'mare semper periculosum est' inquit. 'si Agrippina in mari <u>perierit</u>, nemo te <u>culpabit</u>.' hoc consilium Neroni placuit. ubi navis parata est, Nero matrem <u>Baias</u> ad domum suam invitavit. navem misit ut eam per noctem transportaret.

Agrippina in nave cum duobus amicis sedit. cum navis in medium mare processisset, signo dato tectum decidit. unus ex amicis Agrippinae statim necatus est; ipsa et altera <u>amica</u> in mare iactae sunt.

Names

Baiae, Baiarum (f pl)   Baiae (a seaside resort)

Vocabulary

pereo, perire, perii   I die
culpo, culpare, culpavi, culpatus   I blame
amica, amicae (f)   female friend

[25]

20

V. NERO AND AGRIPPINA

3 Read this final section of the story carefully, then answer all the questions.

*After surviving the first attempt on her life, Agrippina was
killed at the second attempt.*

1 nautae Agrippinam in aqua quaesiverunt. amica eius clamans se
2 Agrippinam esse, necata est. interea Agrippina ipsa tacita ad <u>litus</u> <u>navit</u>; ita
3 domum advenit <u>tuta</u>. cum Nero audivisset matrem <u>adhuc</u> vivere, iratissimus
4 erat. tres milites misit ut eam interficerent. qui cum in domum <u>irrupissent</u>,
5 Agrippina, quamquam perterrita erat, '<u>ventrem</u> <u>ferite</u>' inquit. statim multis
   <u>vulneribus</u> necata est.

Based on Tacitus, Annals XIV.3-9.

Vocabulary

litus, litoris (n)	shore
no, nare, navi	I swim
tutus, tuta, tutum	safe
adhuc	still
irrumpo, irrumpere, irrupi, irruptus	I burst in
venter, ventris (m)	stomach, womb
ferio, ferire	I strike
vulnus, vulneris (n)	wound

(a) *nautae…quaesiverunt* (line 1): what did the sailors do?   [2]
(b) In lines 1-2, what happened to Agrippina's friend?   [3]
(c) How did Agrippina reach safety?   [3]
(d) *cum Nero…erat* (lines 3-4):
   (i) what did Nero hear?   [2]
   (ii) how did he react to this news?   [2]
(e) *tres…interficerent* (line 4): what did Nero do about his mother?   [3]
(f) Describe in detail what happened when the men burst into Agrippina's
   house.   [4]
(g) *'ventrem ferite'* (line 5): suggest a reason why she said this.   [1]

[20]

Total [60]

Higher Tier Tests

VI. *APOLLO AND DAPHNE*

1   Read the first section of the story carefully, then answer all the questions.

Daphne, the beautiful daughter of the river god Peneus,
was pursued by many young men.

  1 <u>Daphne</u> erat filia <u>Penei</u>. puella pulcherrima erat. quamquam multi iuvenes
  2 eam petebant, omnes <u>contemnebat</u>. pater ei saepe dixerat 'debes, o filia,
     maritum filiosque habere.' ea, patrem <u>complexa</u>, semper responderat 'volo
     vitam meam sine viro, sine liberis ducere, carissime pater.' pater invitus
     consenserat. <u>Daphne</u> tamen tam pulchra erat ut iuvenes semper eam
     sequerentur, etiam in silvas, ubi ei maxime placebat ambulare.

Names

Daphne, Daphnes (f) (accusative *Daphnen*)	Daphne
Peneus, Penei (m)	Peneus

Vocabulary

contemno, contemnere, contempsi, contemptus	I reject
complector, complecti, complexus sum	I embrace

(a) In line 1, what **two** details are we given about Daphne?   [2]
(b) *quamquam ... contemnebat* (lines 1-2): describe Daphne's relationship
     with the young men.   [2]
(c) What did Daphne's father think she ought to do?   [2]
(d) How had Daphne reacted to her father's wish? Make **two** points.   [2]
(e) In the last sentence, what would have **(i)** displeased and **(ii)** pleased
     Daphne about the woods?   [2]
                                                    [10]

2 Read this section carefully and then translate it into English. **Please write your translation on alternate lines.**

> *Cupid, the young god of love, made Apollo, the god of archery, fall in love with Daphne, but at the same time he made Daphne reject Apollo.*

olim Apollo, per silvas iter faciens, Cupidinem conspexit. Cupido arcum habebat. Apollo, qui sagittarius optimus erat, eum iussit arcum abicere: 'tu non sagittarius es' inquit 'sed parvus puer.' Cupido iratus sagittam in Apollinem statim misit, ut puellam, quam primam vidit, amaret. ecce! in mediis silvis ambulabat Daphne! simulac eam conspexit, Apollo amore incensus est. ad eam cucurrit, iam in animo vultum crinesque puellae laudans. Cupido autem alteram sagittam habebat, quae amorem deleret; quam in Daphnen misit. ea igitur, cum deum appropinquantem vidisset, fugit. quo celerius Apollo secutus est, eo celerius fugit Daphne. eam orabat ut consisteret, sed puella audire noluit.

Names

Apollo, Apollinis (m)	Apollo
Cupido, Cupidinis (m)	Cupid

Vocabulary

arcus, arcus (m)	bow
sagittarius, sagittarii (m)	archer
sagitta, sagittae (f)	arrow
crinis, crinis (m)	hair
quo ... eo	the more ... the more

[30]

VI. *APOLLO AND DAPHNE*

3 Read this final section of the story carefully, then answer all the questions.

*When Daphne could not escape the pursuing Apollo, she prayed to
her father to help her, with surprising results.*

1 Apollo, dum Daphnen sequitur, 'mane' inquit 'sic <u>cerva</u> leonem fugit. ego
2 te sequor, quod te amo. o me miserum! terra, per quam curris, <u>aspera</u> est.
  curre lentius, lentiusque sequar ego.' timuit enim ne puella decideret.
4 rogavit num sciret quis eam amaret: 'non agricola pauper sum' inquit 'sed
5 filius <u>Iovis</u>.' plura dicere voluit, sed puella iam aberat. Apollo iterum
  amore motus quam celerrime cucurrit, <u>paulatim</u>que propius ad puellam
7 adiit. quae cum iam paene confecta consistere coepisset, aquas fluminis
  conspexit: statim patrem oravit ut adiuvaret. 'muta <u>figuram</u> meam'
  clamavit. his verbis vix dictis, <u>arbor</u> facta est. sed hanc quoque Apollo
10 amavit.   Based on Ovid, *Metamorphoses* I.452-553.

Names

Iuppiter, Iovis (m)   Jupiter

Vocabulary

cerva, cervae (f)	deer
asper, aspera, asperum	rough
paulatim	gradually
muto, mutare, mutavi, mutatus	I change
figura, figurae (f)	shape
arbor, arboris (f)	tree

(a) In line 1, to what event does Apollo liken his pursuit of Daphne? [2]
(b) *ego…amo* (lines 1-2): what argument does Apollo use to try to persuade
   Daphne to stop? [2]
(c) *o me miserum* (line 2):
   (i) what fear prompts Apollo to say this? [2]
   (ii) what compromise does he suggest to Daphne because of this fear? [2]
   (iii) why do you think this suggestion might not be entirely serious? [1]
(d) Lines 4-5:
   (i) how does Apollo try to convince Daphne that he is worthy of her? [2]
   (ii) how much notice did Daphne take of him? [1]
(e) *Apollo ... coepisset* (lines 5-7): explain fully why Apollo began to catch
   up with Daphne. [4]
(f) In lines 7-10, how successful was Daphne in escaping from Apollo's
   attentions? [4]
                                                         [20]

Total [60]

VII. *CAMILLUS AT VEII*

1 Read the first section of the story carefully, then answer all the questions.

The Roman general Camillus found a quick way to
capture the city of Veii.

1 decem iam annos Romani bellum contra <u>Veios</u> gerebant. imperator
2 <u>Camillus</u> urbem capere magnopere volebat. militibus suis magnum
   praemium urbe capta promiserat; etiam deos rogaverat ut auxilium sibi
4 darent. tum <u>Camillus</u> novum consilium cepit: civibus quid faceret
5 nescientibus, <u>cuniculum</u> sub muris urbis facere coepit. dum alii
   Romanorum muros oppugnant, alii per <u>cuniculum</u> in mediam urbem
7 festinaverunt. sic brevi tempore urbs capta est.

Names

Veii, Veiorum (m pl)   Veii
Camillus, Camilli (m)   Camillus

Vocabulary

cuniculus, cuniculi (m)   tunnel

(a) In line 1, what had the Romans been doing, and for how long? [2]
(b) From lines 2-4 (*militibus…darent*), give details of the **two** actions of
       Camillus that show his wish to capture the city. [2 + 2]
(c) *novum consilium* (line 4): what did this involve? [2]
(d) *dum alii…festinaverunt* (lines 5-7): what **two** activities are described here? [2]
                                                                    [10]

VII. CAMILLUS AT VEII

2 Read this section carefully and then translate it into English. **Please write your translation on alternate lines.**

After the capture of Veii, Camillus emptied the city of
people and goods, including the statue of Juno.

Camillus laetus erat, quod urbem Veios tandem ceperat multosque hostium interfecerat. militibus suis, quibus magna praemia promiserat, urbem despoliare permisit. eos cives Veiorum qui etiam vivi erant magno pretio vendidit. omnem pecuniam ita acceptam Romam misit. ex templis quoque omnia auferre coepit. etiam statuam Iunonis cepit. manus autem iuvenum, qui statuam sacram movere iussi erant, timebat ne dea irata esset. unus igitur ex iuvenibus deam adlocutus est: 'visne' inquit 'o regina caeli, Romam nobiscum ire?' statua capite nutare visa est. omnes credebant deam novam domum videre velle. quamquam ingens erat, ad novum templum Romae, a Camillo aedificatum, facile transportata est.

Names

Iuno, Iunonis (f)	Juno

Vocabulary

despolio, despoliare, despoliavi, despoliatus	I plunder
permitto, permittere, permisi, permissus + dat.	I permit
statua, statuae (f)	statue
nuto, nutare, nutavi, nutatus	I nod

[30]

3 Read this final section of the story carefully, then answer all the questions.

Camillus returned to Rome in triumph.

1 ubi Romae nuntiatum est Veios tot post annos captos esse, cives maxime
2 gaudebant, quod bellum tam longum fuerat totque milites occisi erant.
3 feminae ad templa currebant ut deis gratias agerent. magna turba civium
   convenit ad Camillum urbem intrantem salutandum. omnes credebant eum
5 maximum omnium imperatorum esse. ille in tam <u>splendida</u> <u>quadriga</u> in
6 urbem vectus est, ut nonnulli timerent ne deis ipsis <u>aemularetur</u>; etiam inter
   se rogabant num <u>dictator</u> <u>fieri</u> vellet. Camillus autem, duobus novis templis
   deis promissis, imperium suum statim <u>deposuit</u>; credebat enim se omnia
   debita effecisse.

Based on Livy, V.20-3.

Vocabulary

splendidus, splendida, splendidum	splendid
quadriga, quadrigae (f)	four-horse chariot
aemulor, aemulari, aemulatus sum + dat.	I rival
dictator, dictatoris (m)	dictator
fio, fieri, factus sum	I become
depono, deponere, deposui, depositus	I set down, give up

(a) *ubi…occisi erant* (lines 1-2):
    (i) what announcement was made at Rome?   [2]
    (ii) describe and explain the reaction to this announcement.   [1 + 2]
(b) In line 3, how did the women react?   [2]
(c) *magna turba…esse* (lines 3-5):
    (i) explain what the *turba* was doing.   [2]
    (ii) what reason is given for their behaving in this way?   [2]
(d) *ille…vectus est* (lines 5-6):
    (i) show how Camillus' action might have supported the citizens'
beliefs about him.   [2]
    (ii) what **two** fears did this action of Camillus generate among some
citizens?   [2 + 2]
(e) How and why did Camillus show that these fears were groundless?   [2 + 1]

[20]

Total [60]

VIII. *CAMILLUS AT FALERII*

1 Read the first section of the story carefully, then answer all the questions.

Camillus, given command of the Roman forces attacking Falerii
won an early victory.

1 Camillus erat imperator Romanus, qui Veios vicerat. non multo post
    Romani bellum contra Falerios gerebant. cives enim Faleriorum auxilium
3 Veientibus dederant. Romani sperabant Camillum Falerios quoque
4 victurum esse. itaque Camillus milites Falerios duxit. quod hostes ex urbe
5 exire nolebant, Camillus villas frumentumque eorum incendere coepit. sic
    hostes coacti sunt exire, ut haec defenderent. simulatque egressi sunt, victi
    sunt; multis occisis, ceteri rursus in urbem fugerunt.

Names

Camillus, Camilli (m)	Camillus
Veii, Veiorum (m pl)	Veii
Falerii, Faleriorum (m pl)	Falerii
Veiens, Veientis (m)	citizen of Veii

(a)	In line 1, what **two** facts are we given about Camillus?	[2]
(b)	Why were the Romans waging war against Falerii?	[1]
(c)	In lines 3-4, what were the Romans hoping?	[1]
(d)	*quod...coepit* (lines 4-5):	
	(i) what action did Camillus take?	[2]
	(ii) why did he do this?	[2]
(e)	Explain how Camillus' action proved successful.	[2]
		[10]

2 Read this section carefully and then translate it into English. **Please write your translation on alternate lines.**

Expecting a long siege of Falerii, Camillus received a surprise visit from a schoolmaster.

post primam <u>victoriam</u> contra cives Faleriorum, Romani hanc urbem, sicut Veios, <u>obsidere</u> coeperunt. cives tamen, multo frumento iam in urbem portato, priusquam omnes viae <u>clauderentur</u>, multo plus cibi etiam quam Romani habebant. se igitur Romanis non tradiderunt. itaque Camillus credebat se urbem nec facile nec brevi tempore capturum esse. in urbe autem erat <u>magister</u> quidam; quod hic <u>magister</u> optimus erat, pueri, quos docebat, erant filii nobilium. is pueros ex urbe ducere cotidie solebat, ut corpora <u>exercerent</u>. quamquam bellum circum urbem gerebatur, hostes non timebat. olim pueros longius ab urbe ad castra Romanorum duxit. in castra ingressus, ad imperatorem ipsum adiit.

Vocabulary

victoria, victoriae (f)	victory
obsideo, obsidere, obsedi, obsessus	I besiege
claudo, claudere, clausi, clausus	I block, close off
magister, magistri (m)	schoolmaster
exerceo, exercere, exercui, exercitus	I exercise

[30]

VIII. *CAMILLUS AT FALERII*

3 Read this final section of the story carefully, then answer all the questions.

The schoolmaster tried to betray his city.

1 Camillus magistrum rogavit quid vellet et cur venisset. magister respondit
2 se filios omnium nobilium urbis ad Romanos duxisse, ut <u>obsides</u> haberent.
3 'si hos <u>obsides</u> tenebitis' inquit 'mox Falerios capietis; nam patres eorum
   omne imperium in urbe habent. erit nihil quod non facient ad filios
5 recipiendos.' Camillus tamen iratus 'nos Romani' inquit 'talia non
   facimus.' tum <u>virgas</u> omnibus pueris dedit quibus magistrum <u>verberarent</u>.
   turba civium haec a muris urbis spectantium <u>mirata est</u> quanto honore
   Camillus egisset. crediderunt se tam <u>iustos</u> Romanos <u>socios</u> <u>magis</u> quam
   hostes habere malle. ita pax facta est.

Based on Livy, V.26-7.

Vocabulary

obses, obsidis (m)	hostage
virga, virgae (f)	stick, cane
verbero, verberare, verberavi, verberatus	I beat
miror, mirari, miratus sum	I am amazed
iustus, iusta, iustum	just
socius, socii (m)	ally
magis	more, rather

(a) What **two** questions did Camillus ask the schoolmaster? [2]
(b) *magister…haberent* (lines 1-2): what was the schoolmaster's reply? [3]
(c) *si hos…recipiendos* (lines 3-5): how did the schoolmaster explain his
     actions? [4]
(d) Why was Camillus angry at this explanation? [1]
(e) In what way did Camillus punish the schoolmaster? [2]
(f) How did the citizens of Falerii know about the punishment? [2]
(g) What surprised the citizens of Falerii? [2]
(h) Explain fully why the citizens of Falerii made peace. [4]

[20]

Total [60]

IX. PYRAMUS AND THISBE

1 Read the first section of the story carefully, then answer all the questions.

*Pyramus and Thisbe loved each other, but
their parents tried to stop them.*

1 Pyramus et Thisbe in proximis domibus habitabant. Pyramus erat
2 pulcherrimus iuvenis, Thisbe omnium puellarum pulcherrima. primum
3 amici erant, deinde amor eos tenebat. quamquam matrimonium cupiebant,
4 patres matresque eos convenire vetuerunt. sed tanto amore incensi sunt ut
5 saepe signa inter se darent. nam forte erat parva rima per murum qui duas
   domus dividebat. hanc rimam, multos annos a nullo conspectam, amantes
7 tandem invenerunt.

Names

Pyramus, Pyrami (m)	Pyramus
Thisbe, Thisbes (acc. *Thisben*) (f)	Thisbe

Vocabulary

matrimonium, matrimonii (n)	marriage
veto, vetare, vetui, vetitus	I forbid
rima, rimae (f)	crack
divido, dividere, divisi, divisus	I divide, separate

(a) In the first sentence, what information are we given about where Pyramus
and Thisbe lived?   [1]

(b) *Pyramus…pulcherrima* (lines 1-2): in what way were the two similar?   [1]

(c) *primum…tenebat* (lines 2-3): how did their relationship develop?   [2]

(d) *quamquam…vetuerunt* (lines 3-4): why could they not continue to
develop their relationship?   [2]

(e) **(i)** Describe the *rima* (lines 5-7).   [3]

   (ii) How could the *rima* help Pyramus and Thisbe?   [1]

[10]

IX. PYRAMUS AND THISBE

2 Read this section carefully and then translate it into English. **Please write your translation on alternate lines.**

The two lovers eventually agreed to meet
at night by Ninius' tomb.

Pyramus Thisbeque per rimam <u>cotidie</u> loquebantur. saepe 'o mure' inquiunt 'cur nobis amantibus <u>obstas</u>?' ubi nox veniebat, <u>osculis</u> muro datis tristes abibant. deinde, quod eadem facere non diutius volebant, constituerunt e domibus <u>furtim</u> nocte egressi ad locum quendam convenire: hic locus erat <u>bustum</u> <u>Nini</u>, ubi <u>arbor</u> prope <u>fontem</u> erat. cum Thisbe, media nocte profecta, ad <u>bustum</u> prima advenisset, sub <u>arbore</u> sedebat ad Pyramum exspectandum. subito leo, cuius vultus <u>oblitus</u> sanguine erat, <u>fonti</u> appropinquavit ut aquam biberet. Thisbe, simulac leonem conspexit, in <u>antrum</u> fugiens <u>velamen</u> suum in terra reliquit. quod visum leo tam <u>violenter</u> <u>dilaniavit</u> ut multum sanguinis in eo relinqueret.

Names

Ninius, Nini (m)   Ninius

Vocabulary

cotidie	every day
obsto, obstare, obstiti + dat.	I stand in the way (of)
osculum, osculi (n)	kiss
furtim	secretly
bustum, busti (n)	tomb
arbor, arboris (f)	tree
fons, fontis (m)	spring
oblitus, oblita, oblitum	smeared
antrum, antri (n)	cave
velamen, velaminis (n)	veil
violenter	violently
dilanio, dilaniare, dilaniavi, dilaniatus	I tear apart

[30]

3 Read this final section of the story carefully, then answer all the questions.

The two would-be lovers died.

ubi Pyramus non multo post advenit, et <u>vestigia</u> leonis et velamen
dilaniatum invenit. quod credidit Thisben mortuam esse, exclamavit se
3 quoque moriturum esse. gladio quem secum ferebat se <u>transfixit</u>. sanguis
4 morientis e vulnere fusus est. iam Thisbe, quae timebat ne Pyramo
adveniente abesset, ad arborem rediit. corpus Pyrami in terra iacens
perterrita vidit. amantem <u>amplexa</u>, lacrimas <u>super</u> vulnus eius fudit. tum
velamine <u>agnito</u> conspectoque gladio, intellexit quid accidisset. 'ad
mortem' inquit 'te sequar. si in eadem domo non habitabimus, in eodem
busto iacebimus.' gladio sub <u>pectus</u> posito, <u>prolapsa est</u>.

Based on Ovid, Metamorphoses IV.55-166.

Vocabulary

vestigium, vestigii (n)	footprint
transfigo, transfigere, transfixi, transfixus	I stab
amplector, amplecti, amplexus sum	I embrace
super + acc.	on top of
agnosco, agnoscere, agnovi, agnitus	I recognise
pectus, pectoris (n)	breast
prolabor, prolabi, prolapsus sum	I fall forward

(a) What **two** things did Pyramus see when he arrived? [2]
(b) What did he decide to do, and why? [2]
(c) *gladio...fusus est* (lines 3-4): describe Pyramus' death. [3]
(d) Why did Thisbe return to the tree? [2]
(e) What terrified Thisbe? [2]
(f) How did Thisbe show her grief? [3]
(g) How did Thisbe work out what had happened? [2]
(h) (i)   What did Thisbe decide to do? [1]
     (ii) What reason did she give for her decision? [2]
(i) How did Thisbe die? [1]

[20]

Total [60]

X. GHOSTS

1   Read the first section of the story carefully, then answer all the questions.

Curtius Rufus received good and bad predictions.

1   <u>Curtius Rufus</u> erat vir nobilis qui in <u>Africa</u> habitabat. in <u>porticu</u> domus suae
ambulabat. <u>figura</u> feminae apparuit, magna et pulchra. illa <u>Rufo</u> perterrito
dixit se deam <u>Africam</u> esse et quae futura essent <u>praenuntiare</u> posse. 'tu'
inquit 'Romam ibis ubi honores accipies. tum summo cum imperio in hanc
eandem <u>provinciam</u> revenies, et hic morieris.' eadem <u>figura</u> ei ad <u>Africam</u>
regresso egredientique e nave apparuit. mox mortuus est.

Names

Curtius Rufus, Curtii Rufi (m)	Curtius Rufus
Africa, Africae (f)	Africa (both province and goddess)

Vocabulary

porticus, porticus (m)	portico, colonnade
figura, figurae (f)	figure
praenuntio, praenuntiare, praenuntiavi, praenuntiatus	I predict
provincia, provinciae (f)	province

(a)   From line 1, give **one** detail about Curtius Rufus.   [1]
(b)   Describe what Curtius saw while walking in the colonnade.   [2]
(c)   Pick out the Latin word which tells us how Curtius reacted to what he saw.   [1]
(d)   What did the figure predict?   [4]
(e)   When did Curtius see the figure again?   [2]

[10]

2   Read this section carefully and then translate it into English. **Please write your translation on alternate lines.**

Athenodorus bought a house in Athens, despite knowing that it was haunted.

erat <u>Athenis</u> domus magna sed <u>infamis</u>; nam per <u>silentium</u> noctis sonitus ferri audiri poterat. mox apparebat <u>imago</u> senis <u>vincula</u> in manibus gerentis. ei qui in domo habitabant noctes tam diras per <u>timorem</u> habebant ut numquam dormirent; mors sequebatur. mox domus <u>deserta</u> erat, quod nemo eam emere volebat. deinde <u>Athenodorus</u> <u>philosophus</u> <u>Athenas</u> venit, ut domum sibi emeret. hac domo visa pretioque audito, quamquam <u>imaginem</u> ibi esse cognoverat, pecuniam tradidit. ubi nox erat, servos iussit <u>pugillares</u> in primam partem domus ferre; ibi scribere coepit. primo erat <u>silentium</u>; deinde <u>vincula</u> moveri audita sunt. <u>Athenodorus</u> oculis non sublatis scribebat. tum sonitus maior propiorque fuit.

Names

Athenae, Athenarum (f pl)	Athens
Athenodorus, Athenodori (m)	Athenodorus

Vocabulary

infamis, infamis, infame	infamous, disreputable
silentium, silentii (n)	silence
imago, imaginis (f)	image, ghost
vinculum, vinculi (n)	chain
timor, timoris (m)	fear
desertus, deserta, desertum	deserted
philosophus, philosophi (m)	philosopher
pugillares, pugillarium (m pl)	writing tablets

[30]

X. GHOSTS

3 Read this final section of the story carefully, then answer all the questions.

Athenodorus was not frightened by a visit from the ghost.

1 Athenodorus, ubi tandem oculos sustulit, imaginem vidit, sicut narrata erat;
2 quae prope ianuam stans signum manu faciebat. philosophus tamen, nullo
3 modo territus, imagini imperavit ut exspectaret, rursusque scribere coepit.
4 imago ei appropinquavit et vincula <u>super</u> caput scribentis <u>quassit</u>. ille e
5 <u>lecto</u> tandem surrexit, ut imaginem sequeretur. in hortum lente ductus est.
6 ibi imago <u>dilapsa est</u>. postridie Athenodorus servis imperavit ut illum
7 locum <u>effoderent</u>: credidit enim corpus hominis mortui ibi iacere. <u>ossa</u>
invenerunt vinculis <u>inserta</u>; quae <u>collecta</u> in <u>sepulcro</u> a sacerdote <u>sepulta</u>
sunt. numquam postea imago visa est.

Based on Pliny, *Letters* VII.27.

Vocabulary

super + acc.	above
quatio, quatere, quassi, quassus	I shake
lectus, lecti (m)	couch
dilabor, dilabi, dilapsus sum	I disappear
effodio, effodere, effodi, effossus	I dig up, excavate
os, ossis (n)	bone
insero, inserere, inserui, insertus + dat.	I enclose within
colligo, colligere, collegi, collectus	I collect
sepulcrum, sepulcri (n)	tomb, grave
sepelio, sepelire, sepelivi, sepultus	I bury

(a) *Athenodorus…faciebat* (lines 1-2): decribe in detail what Athenodorus saw when he raised his eyes. [4]
(b) *philosophus…coepit* (lines 2-3): what was Athenodorus' reaction to what he saw? [3]
(c) In line 4, what **two** things did the ghost do? [2]
(d) How did Athenodorus respond now to the ghost's actions? [3]
(e) Suggest a reason why the ghost might have moved *lente* (line 5). [1]
(f) *postridie…iacere* (lines 6-7):
    (i) what order did Athenodorus give the next morning? [2]
    (ii) why did he give this order? [2]
(g) Explain fully why the ghost was never seen again after this episode. [3]

[20]

Total [60]

XI. DEIPHOBUS

1 Read the first section of the story carefully, then answer all the questions.

*While visiting the Underworld, Aeneas saw the spirit of
his old friend, Deiphobus.*

Aeneas erat dux Troianorum. in Tartarum descenderat ut patrem videret,
qui iam mortuus erat. dum inter manes ambulat, Aeneas Deiphobum
3 conspexit: qui multis ante annis amicus eius fuerat sed occisus erat Troiam
4 contra Graecos defendens. quo conspecto Aeneas perterritus erat, non
solum quod nesciebat eum mortuum esse, sed etiam quod species dira erat:
nam nec nasum neque aures habebat.

Names

Aeneas, Aeneae (acc. *Aenean*) (m)	Aeneas
Troiani, Troianorum (m pl)	Trojans
Tartarus, Tartari (m)	the Underworld
Deiphobus, Deiphobi (m)	Deiphobus
Troia, Troiae (f)	Troy
Graeci, Graecorum (m pl)	Greeks

Vocabulary

manes, manium (m pl)	spirits (of the dead)
species, speciei (f)	appearance
nasus, nasi (m)	nose
auris, auris (f)	ear

(a)	Who was Aeneas?	[1]
(b)	Why had Aeneas entered the Underworld?	[1]
(c)	What was Aeneas doing when he saw Deiphobus?	[1]
(d)	*qui...defendens* (lines 3-4): what information is given here about Deiphobus?	[4]
(e)	Explain fully why Aeneas was terrified by the sight of Deiphobus.	[3]

[10]

XI. *DEIPHOBUS*

2 Read this section carefully and then translate it into English. **Please write your translation on alternate lines.**

> *Deiphobus blamed Helen for his wounds;*
> *Helen had been married three times.*

Aeneas ad Deiphobum adiit. eum rogavit quid accidisset. 'in urbe' inquit
Aeneas 'audivi te fortissime pugnavisse. te invenire conatus sum, sed non
potui. sed quis haec fecit?' ille respondit Aenean plura facere non potuisse.
'Helena erat' inquit 'quae haec fecit.' eo tempore Helena erat uxor
Deiphobi, sed multis ante annis uxor fuerat Menelai, regis Graeci. quod
haec femina pulcherrima erat, dea Venus eam Paridi dederat; qui Venerem
omnium dearum pulcherrimam esse iudicaverat. 'illa nocte' inquit
Deiphobus 'postquam equum ligneum in urbem traximus, omnes
gaudebamus. nam credidimus Graecos abiisse bellumque confectum esse.
feminae per urbem saltabant, interque eas Helena, facem tenens.'

Names

Helena, Helenae (f)	Helen
Menelaus, Menelai (m)	Menelaus
Graecus, Graeca, Graecum	Greek
Venus, Veneris (f)	Venus
Paris, Paridis (m)	Paris (a Trojan prince)

Vocabulary

iudico, iudicare, iudicavi, iudicatus	I judge
ligneus, lignea, ligneum	wooden
salto, saltare, saltavi, saltatus	I dance
fax, facis (f)	torch

[30]

3 Read this final section of the story carefully, then answer all the questions.

Deiphobus related how Helen betrayed him and his city.

1 Deiphobus Aeneae narrabat quo modo necatus esset. 'illa fax, quam ceteri
credebamus lucem saltantibus ferre, fuit signum Graecis, qui in navibus
3 ad urbem oppugnandam id exspectabant. dum hostes Troiam ingrediuntur,
4 ego ignarus domum ivi ut dormirem. Helena, mea optima uxor, omnibus
5 armis meis e domo elatis, ianuaque aperta, Menelaum in domum invitavit.
6 qui cum amicis, gladiis strictis, in cubiculum cucurrit. ego, qui eis resistere
7 non diu potui, haec vulnera passus sum. nunc hic habito, semper cum
eisdem vulneribus.' quibus dictis deos oravit ut Graecos atque ante omnes
Helenam eodem modo punirent.

Based on Virgil, Aeneid VI.494-529.

Vocabulary

arma, armorum (n pl)	arms, weapons
stringo, stringere, strinxi, strictus	I draw (a sword)
cubiculum, cubiculi (n)	bedroom

(a) In line 1, what was Deiphobus doing? [2]
(b) *illa fax…exspectabant* (lines 1-3):
   (i) how was the torch wrongly interpreted? [2]
   (ii) what was the torch really for? [3]
(c) *ego…dormirem* (line 4): what did Deiphobus do, and why? [2]
(d) *mea optima uxor* (line 4): why do you think Deiphobus described his
wife as *optima*? [1]
(e) *Helena…invitavit* (lines 4-5): what **three** things did Helen do to betray
her husband? [3]
(f) *qui…passus sum* (lines 6-7): describe the sequence of events in the
bedroom. [3]
(g) In death, what had not changed for Deiphobus? [1]
(h) What prayer did Deiphobus make at the end? [3]

[20]

Total [60]

XII. *AESCULAPIUS COMES TO ROME*

1 Read the first section of the story carefully, then answer all the questions.

A plague forced the Romans to seek help from Apollo,
who directed them to his son.

olim <u>pestilentia</u> dira multos Romanos necabat. quod nihil contra hanc ipsi
facere poterant, auxilium a deis petiverunt. <u>legatos Delphos</u> miserunt ut
<u>oraculum Apollinis</u> audirent. e medio templo haec vox audita est: 'non ad
me sed ad filium meum adire debetis, Romani.' cum haec Romam
5 rettulissent, senatores <u>legatos</u> iterum emiserunt, qui domum filii <u>Apollinis</u>,
6 <u>Aesculapii</u> nomine, quaererent. mox cognoverunt eum <u>Epidauri</u> habitare.

Names

Delphi, Delphorum (m pl)	Delphi (a holy site in Greece)
Apollo, Apollinis (m)	Apollo
Aesculapius, Aesculapii (m)	Aesculapius
Epidaurus, Epidauri (f)	Epidaurus (a city in Greece)

Vocabulary

pestilentia, pestilentiae (f)	plague
legatus, legati (m	(here) ambassador
oraculum, oraculi (n)	oracle, prophecy

(a)	In the first sentence, what effect was the plague having?	[2]
(b)	Why were the Romans forced to seek help against the plague?	[2]
(c)	Why did the Romans send ambassadors to Delphi?	[1]
(d)	What advice did the ambassadors receive?	[2]
(e)	In lines 5-6, why were the ambassadors sent out again?	[2]
(f)	What success did this second embassy have?	[1]

[10]

2   Read this section carefully and then translate it into English. **Please write your translation on alternate lines.**

> *The Romans tried to persuade the people of Epidaurus*
> *to give them their god.*

Romani, simulac cognoverunt Aesculapium Epidauri habitare, navem trans mare ad illam urbem miserunt. in nave erant legati eorum. postquam legati Epidaurum intraverunt, <u>decuriones</u> arcessitos oraverunt ut deum suum Romanis darent, qui populum morientem servaret. alii <u>decuriones</u> statim consenserunt, alii deum tradere noluerunt. per totum diem ita <u>contenderunt</u>. illa nocte, dum omnes dormiunt, Aesculapius uni ex legatis in <u>somnio</u> apparuit, <u>sceptrum</u> tenens. 'noli timere' inquit; '<u>imagine</u> mea hic relicta, ipse libenter vobiscum veniam. hanc <u>serpentem</u> specta, quae circum <u>sceptrum</u> meum est; sic me cognoscere poteris: nam ego in talem <u>serpentem</u> me vertam, sed maior hac ero.' his verbis dictis deus abiit.

Vocabulary

decurio, decurionis (m)	town councillor
contendo, contendere, contendi, contentus	(here) I argue
somnium, somnii (n)	dream
sceptrum, sceptri (n)	sceptre
imago, imaginis (f)	image, likeness
serpens, serpentis (f)	serpent, snake

[30]

XII. *AESCULAPIUS COMES TO ROME*

3 Read this final section of the story carefully, then answer all the questions.

*The god appeared as a snake and sailed with
the Romans to Rome.*

1 postridie decuriones ad templum dei convenerunt, ut signum e caelo
2 peterent. statim ingens serpens apparuit. oculi eius adeo <u>fulgebant</u> ut omnes
cives terrerentur. sacerdos tamen, qui deum <u>agnovit</u>, omnibus imperavit ut
4 tacerent. tum et cives et Romani deum <u>venerati sunt</u>. serpens, cum capite
5 <u>nutavisset</u>, a templo, ubi tam diu habitaverat, discessit. per mediam urbem
ad portum <u>lapsa</u>, in navem Romanam se posuit. Romani gaudentes navem
<u>solverunt</u>. post sex dies prima luce Romam redierunt. totus populus urbis
ad <u>ripas</u> fluminis ad deum salutandum convenit; qui sine <u>mora</u> pestilentiam
<u>expulit</u>.

Based on Ovid, Metamorphoses XV.626-744.

Vocabulary

fulgeo, fulgere, fulsi	I shine, gleam
agnosco, agnoscere, agnovi, agnitus	I recognise
veneror, venerari, veneratus sum	I worship
nuto, nutare, nutavi, nutatus	I nod
labor, labi, lapsus sum	I glide
solvo, solvere, solvi, solutus	I launch
ripa, ripae (f)	bank
mora, morae (f)	delay
expello, expellere, expuli, expulsus	I drive out, get rid of

(a) In lines 1-2, where did the town councillors meet, and why? [1 + 2]
(b) From line 2, give **two** facts about the *serpens*. [2]
(c) Describe the intervention of the priest. [2]
(d) How did those present react to the priest's intervention? [2]
(e) *cum capite nutavisset* (lines 4-5): why do you think the *serpens* did this? [1]
(f) Describe fully the serpent's journey to the ship. [4]
(g) When exactly did the ship reach Rome? [2]
(h) (i) How did the Romans welcome the god? [2]
　　(ii) How did the god respond? [2]

[20]

Total [60]

XIII. *THESEUS AND ARIADNE*

1 Read the first section of the story carefully, then answer all the questions.

Theseus volunteered to fight the Minotaur.

Minos erat rex Cretae. postquam filius eius Athenis interfectus est,
Atheniensibus imperavit ut poenas darent: iussit eos septem puellas
septemque iuvenes ad Cretam mittere, ut Minotaurus eos consumeret. rex
Atheniensium filium habebat, Theseum nomine; qui ipse ire constituit, ut
Minotauro occiso ceteros servaret. pater autem eius, qui timebat ne ipse a
monstro occideretur, ei persuadere ne iret frustra conatus est.

Names

Minos, Minois (m)	Minos
Creta, Cretae (f)	Crete
Athenae, Athenarum (f pl)	Athens
Athenienses, Atheniensium (m pl)	Athenians
Minotaurus, Minotauri (m)	Minotaur (a half-human monster)
Theseus, Thesei (m)	Theseus

Vocabulary

monstrum, monstri (n)	monster

(a)	Who was Minos?	[1]
(b)	Why was Minos annoyed with the people of Athens?	[1]
(c)	What punishment did Minos demand of the Athenians?	[3]
(d)	Who was Theseus?	[1]
(e)	What did Theseus decide to do?	[3]
(f)	Why did Theseus' father try to persuade him to change his mind?	[1]

[10]

XIII. *THESEUS AND ARIADNE*

2 Read this section carefully and then translate it into English. **Please write your translation on alternate lines.**

> *Theseus followed a ball of magic wool, which unrolled*
> *before him to lead him to the Minotaur.*

Theseus Athenis cum ceteris Atheniensibus discessit. ubi ad portum Cretae advenerunt, Minos rex eos ad <u>regiam</u> suam duxit. antequam in <u>labyrinthum</u>, in quo Minotaurus habitabat, ducti sunt, cenam consumpserunt. <u>iuxta</u> Theseum sedebat <u>Ariadna</u>, filia Minois. ea simulac iuvenem conspexit, amavit. post cenam igitur <u>Ariadna</u> ad Theseum venit, gladium <u>lanam</u>que ferens. quibus Theseo traditis, promisit se ad <u>labyrinthum</u> postridie venturam esse ad eos liberandos. in <u>labyrintho</u>, ceteris prope ianuam relictis, Theseus <u>lanam</u> <u>proiectam</u> secutus est dum in medium <u>labyrinthum</u> ad Minotaurum adveniret. quamquam monstrum tam dirum numquam antea viderat, gladio facile superavit. cum ad ceteros rediisset, exspectaverunt dum <u>Ariadna</u> eos liberaret.

Names

Ariadna, Ariadnae (f)   Ariadne

Vocabulary

regia, regiae (f)   palace
labyrinthus, labyrinthi (m)   labyrinth
iuxta + acc   next to
lana, lanae (f)   wool
proicio, proicere, proieci, proiectus   I throw ahead

[30]

3 Read this final section of the story carefully, then answer all the questions.

Ariadne had two surprises in one morning.

1 Ariadna Athenienses liberatos e regia ad portum duxit. navem celeriter
2 <u>conscenderunt</u> <u>solverunt</u>que. multas post horas ad insulam <u>Naxum</u>
3 venerunt. hic, quod nox erat omnesque fessi erant, nave ex aqua tracta
4 dormiverunt. Ariadna iuxta Theseum laeta iacebat. postridie tamen
Ariadna, ubi <u>experrecta est</u>, erat sola; <u>collem</u> ascendit ut <u>circumspiceret</u>:
6 neminem vidit. tum intellexit Athenienses nocte abiisse. et miserrima et
7 iratissima erat, quod Theseo amorem atque auxilium suum libenter dederat.
dum se rogat quid faceret, deus <u>Bacchus</u> eam a caelo conspectam amavit.
mox Ariadna Thesei <u>oblita est</u>: uxor enim <u>Bacchi</u> erat.

Based on Catullus, *LXIV*.

Names

Naxos, Naxi (f) Naxos
Bacchus, Bacchi (m) Bacchus

Vocabulary

conscendo, conscendere, conscendi, conscensus I board
solvo, solvere, solvi, solutus I launch, cast off
expergiscor, expergisci, experrectus sum I wake up
collis, collis (m) hill
circumspicio, circumspicere, circumspexi,
  circumspectus I look round
obliviscor, oblivisci, oblitus sum + gen. I forget

(a) In line 1, what **two** things did Ariadne do? [2]
(b) *multas…venerunt* (lines 2-3): describe their journey. [2]
(c) Why did they stop sailing? [2]
(d) What did they have to do before they slept? [2]
(e) Where did Ariadne sleep? [1]
(f) *postridie…vidit* (lines 4-6): what happened the next morning? [3]
(g) *tum…dederat* (lines 6-7): describe and explain Ariadne's state of mind. [4]
(h) How does the story end happily for Ariadne? [4]

[20]

Total [60]

XIV. *ATTACK ON ROME*

1   Read the first section of the story carefully, then answer all the questions.

A conspiracy was formed to restore Tarquinius to
the throne of Rome.

    olim <u>Tarquinius</u> erat rex Romae. hic vir erat crudelis. post multos annos
    civis quidam, <u>Brutus</u> nomine, eum ex urbe <u>expulit</u>. deinde <u>Brutus</u> primus
3 <u>consul</u> Romae factus est. pauci tamen iuvenes <u>Tarquinium</u> redire volebant,
4 quod regem quam <u>consulem</u> habere malebant. dum consilia faciunt, servus
    omnia audita ad <u>Brutum</u> rettulit; qui iuvenes rapi iussit. inter iuvenes autem
    erant duo filii <u>Bruti</u>.

Names

Tarquinius, Tarquinii (m)	Tarquinius
Brutus, Bruti (m)	Brutus

Vocabulary

expello, expellere, expuli, expulsus	I drive out, expel
consul, consulis (m)	consul (high-ranking statesman)

(a)	What sort of a man was Tarquinius?	[1]
(b)	What happened to Tarquinius after many years?	[1]
(c)	What happened to Brutus afterwards?	[1]
(d)	*pauci...malebant* (lines 3-4):	
	(i) what was the conspiracy?	[2]
	(ii) what was the reason for the conspiracy?	[2]
(e)	How did Brutus learn of the conspiracy?	[2]
(f)	What problem did the conspiracy cause for Brutus?	[1]

[10]

2 Read this section carefully and then translate it into English. **Please write your translation on alternate lines.**

> *Brutus, after condemning his sons to death,*
> *died himself in battle against Tarquinius.*

iam Brutus <u>quaestionem</u> habuit. inter <u>reos</u> erant duo filii eius. Brutus, qui maximum imperium in urbe habebat, filios servare potuit; sed eos non liberavit. populus enim imperium ei dederat, quod <u>probissimus</u> erat. constituit igitur non filios sed Romam servandam esse. itaque filios <u>sontes</u> cum ceteris iuvenibus interfici iussit. iam cives Bruto etiam maiores honores dederunt. Tarquinius, cum <u>coniurationem</u> cognitam esse audivisset, iratus erat. nam imperium Romae iterum habere cupiebat. urbem oppugnare ei placuit. postquam aliis urbibus persuasit ut auxilium darent, cum ingenti <u>exercitu</u> Romam contendit. in <u>proelio</u> et filius Tarquinii et Brutus necati sunt. hostibus a Tarquinio abductis, Romani gaudebant.

Vocabulary

quaestio, quaestionis (f)	trial
reus, rei (m)	defendant
probus, proba, probum	honest
sons, sontis	guilty
coniuratio, coniurationis (f)	conspiracy
exercitus, exercitus (m)	army
proelium, proelii (n)	battle

[30]

XIV. ATTACK ON ROME

3 Read this final section of the story carefully, then answer all the questions.

*A second attack on Rome was defeated by
the bravery of Horatius Cocles.*

1 mox Tarquinius Romam capere cum etiam maiore exercitu conatus est.
2 urbem obsidebant. erat pons ligneus qui viam trans flumen in urbem
3 ferebat. quamquam custodes fortissimi hunc pontem noctes diesque
   custodiebant, timebant ne hostes eum caperent. proelio feroci coepto,
5 Romani perterriti trans pontem in urbem fugerunt. dux militum pontem
6 custodientium erat Horatius Cocles. is, simulatque ultimi fugientium
   pontem transierunt, suis imperavit ut pontem celeriter delerent. interea ipse
8 in medio ponte stetit, gladium tenens, unus contra plurimos. hostibus
   oppugnantibus facile restitit. tandem clamoribus militum pontem delentium
   auditis, Horatius in aquam desiluit. urbs tuta erat.

Based on Livy, II.1-10.

Names

Horatius Cocles (m)   Horatius Cocles

Vocabulary

obsideo, obsidere, obsedi, obsessus   I besiege
ligneus, lignea, ligneum   wooden
desilio, desilire, desilui   I jump down

(a) *mox...conatus est* (line 1): give details of the second attack on Rome. [2]
(b) In lines 2-3, what was the function of the bridge? [2]
(c) *custodes* (line 3): what information is given about these? [2]
(d) What fear did the *custodes* have? [1]
(e) In line 5, what was the outcome of the battle? [2]
(f) What was the responsibility of Horatius Cocles? [2]
(g) *is...plurimos* (lines 6-8): give full details of Horatius' plan. [5]
(h) How did Horatius' plan prove successful? [4]

[20]

Total [60]

XV. THE ROPE

1 Read the first section of the story carefully, then answer all the questions.

A ship carrying the slave-girl Palaestra was
wrecked in a storm.

1 olim navis trans mare navigabat. in nave erat pulcherrima puella, Palaestra
2 nomine. Palaestra ancilla erat. dominus eius erat Labrax, homo pessimus.
   quamquam iuvenis quidam ancillam emere cupiens multam pecuniam ei
   dederat, Labrax eam procul a patria vendere volebat. media nocte tanta
   tempestas fuit ut navis in scopulos pelleretur. dum navis mergitur, puella in
   mare desiluit et ad terram vix viva advenit.

Names

Palaestra, Palaestrae (f)   Palaestra
Labrax, Labracis (m)   Labrax

Vocabulary

patria, patriae (f)   native land
scopulus, scopuli (m)   rock
pello, pellere, pepuli, pulsus   I drive
mergo, mergere, mersi, mersus   I sink
desilio, desilire, desilui   I jump down

(a) In line 1, where was the ship sailing?   [1]
(b) In line 1, how is the girl described?   [1]
(c) From line 2, give **two** details about Labrax.   [2]
(d) How was Labrax trying to cheat the young man?   [2]
(e) What was the effect of the storm?   [1]
(f) What happened to the girl at the end of the passage?   [3]

[10]

XV. *THE ROPE*

2   Read this section carefully and then translate it into English. **Please write your translation on alternate lines.**

Palaestra sought help at a temple,
but Labrax found her there.

prope mare erat templum <u>Veneris</u>. forte Labrax promiserat se Palaestram
ad templum ducturum esse ut iuveni traderet. hic iuvenis ancillam emere
voluerat quod eam magnopere amabat. iam puella sola erat, nesciebatque
quid faceret. erat prope templum parva villa, in qua senex habitabat. hic
senex multis ante annis filiam suam amiserat: nam a <u>latronibus</u> capta ablata
erat. is quoque iam solus cum paucis servis habitabat. puella templum
ingressa sacerdotem oravit ut se adiuvaret. interea Labrax, qui e nave
quoque effugerat, ad templum appropinquavit. puellam conspectam capere
conatus est. senex, clamoribus in templo auditis, puellam servavit; duobus
servis imperavit ut Labracem tenerent.

Names

Venus, Veneris (f)   Venus

Vocabulary

latro, latronis (m)   robber

[30]

3 Read this final section of the story carefully, then answer all the questions.

*A slave provided the means for Palaestra to
prove her freeborn status.*

1 dum omnes prope templum stant, <u>Gripus</u>, qui servus senis erat, advenit.
2 <u>rudentem</u> tenebat, quo <u>arcam</u> per terram trahebat. hanc <u>arcam</u> in mari
3 invenerat. Labrax <u>arcam</u> <u>agnovit</u>, quod in nave eam ipse posuerat. hac
4 conspecta, Palaestra laetissima fuit, quod scivit <u>crepundia</u> sua in ea inesse.
5 cum enim capta esset, ea secum habebat. 'haec <u>crepundia</u>' inquit 'quibus
6 olim <u>ludebam</u>, ostendent me <u>liberam</u>, non ancillam esse.' omnia <u>descripsit</u>
7 priusquam Gripus ea ex <u>arca</u> extraxit. senex quoque, qui haec spectabat,
8 <u>crepundia</u> <u>agnovit</u>: nam filia eius talia habuerat. iam intellexit Palaestram illam
9 filiam esse. omnes maxime gaudebant.   Based on Plautus, *The Rope*.

Names

Gripus, Gripi (m)   Gripus

Vocabulary

rudens, rudentis (m)	rope
arca, arcae (f)	chest, large box
agnosco, agnoscere, agnovi, agnitus	I recognise
crepundia, crepundiorum (n pl)	toys
ludo, ludere, lusi, lusus	I play
liber, libera, liberum	free
describo, describere, descripsi, descriptus	I describe

(a) *dum…advenit* (line 1):
    (i) what was everyone doing?   [2]
    (ii) who was Gripus?   [1]
(b) In line 2, what was Gripus doing?   [3]
(c) Explain how the *arca* came to be in the sea.   [2]
(d) *hac conspecta…inesse* (lines 3-4): describe and explain Palaestra's
reaction to seeing the *arca*.   [2]
(e) *cum enim…esse* (lines 5-6): why were the *crepundia* especially important
to Palaestra?   [3]
(f) *omnia…extraxit* (lines 6-7): how did Palaestra show that she owned the
crepundia?   [2]
(g) In lines 8-9, how did the old man react?   [4]
(h) How does the story end?   [1]

[20]

Total [60]

XVI. AENEAS SEEKS A NEW HOME I

1 Read the first section of the story carefully, then answer all the questions.

*The survivors of the Trojan War left Troy and prepared to sail in
search of a new home under the leadership of Aeneas.*

1 illa nocte ubi <u>Graeci</u> urbem ceperunt, omnes <u>Troiani</u>, qui non interfecti
2 erant, in <u>agros</u> prope urbem convenerunt. aderant non solum multi viri
   multaeque feminae, sed etiam liberi et senes. parati erant <u>Aenean</u> ad novam
   terram sequi. cum trans montem <u>Idam</u> ivissent, prima luce ad mare
5 advenerunt. navibus ibi aedificatis, tandem profecti sunt, lacrimantes quod
6 numquam iterum patriam visuri erant.

Names

Graeci, Graecorum (m pl)	Greeks
Troiani, Troianorum (m pl)	Trojans
Aeneas, Aeneae (m) (accusative *Aenean*)	Aeneas
Ida, Idae (f)	Ida (a mountain near Troy)

Vocabulary

ager, agri (m)	field

(a) In line 1, what did the Greeks do?   [1]

(b) **(i)** In lines 1-2, which Trojans are mentioned?   [1]

     (ii) Where did they meet?   [2]

(c) Besides men and women, who else were present?   [2]

(d) Describe the journey the Trojans made.   [2]

(e) In lines 5-6, why were the Trojans crying?   [2]

   [10]

2   Read this section carefully and then translate it into English. **Please write your translation on alternate lines.**

> *The Trojans, after hearing a prophecy from the god Apollo, decided to sail to the island of Crete to make a new home for themselves.*

Aeneas et Troiani multos dies navigabant. postquam ad parvam insulam advenerunt, ubi templum <u>Apollinis</u> erat, deum oraverunt ut novam domum sibi daret. subito vox e terra surgere audita est: 'redire debetis, o Troiani, ad illam terram, in qua primum habitabatis. quaerite <u>antiquam</u> matrem: hic enim magnum imperium habebitis.' Troiani gaudentes inter se rogabant, ubi esset haec terra. pater Aeneae, iam senex, 'audite' inquit 'o duces Troiani, et cognoscite id quod sperare potestis. in medio mari iacet insula <u>Creta</u>, ubi stat alter mons Ida. pater noster primus, <u>Teucer</u>, <u>inde</u> ad <u>Asiam</u> navigavit, ut <u>regnum</u> Troianum <u>constitueret</u>. itaque <u>Creta</u> nobis petenda est.'

Names

Apollo, Apollinis (m)	Apollo
Creta, Cretae (f)	Crete
Teucer, Teucri (m)	Teucer
Asia, Asiae (f)	Asia

Vocabulary

antiquus, antiqua, antiquum	ancient, former
inde	from there
regnum, regni (n)	kingdom
constituo, constituere, constitui, constitutus	I establish

[30]

XVI. AENEAS SEEKS A NEW HOME I

3 Read this final section of the story carefully, then answer all the questions.

*Their new home on Crete proved a failure, and so
they had to set sail again.*

1 Aeneas igitur suos trans mare iterum duxit. tribus post diebus, cum ad <u>oras</u>
2 Cretae advenissent, <u>moenia</u> novae urbis aedificare statim coeperunt. brevi
3 tempore multae domus confectae erant, forum ac templa parabantur. deinde
   tamen <u>pestilentia</u> tam dira et homines et frumentum oppugnavit, ut plurimi
5 Troianorum morerentur. tum media nocte deus quidam Aeneae in <u>somnio</u>
6 apparuit, in luce lunae plenae stans: dixit <u>pestilentiam</u> a deis missam esse;
7 se Troianos ad Italiam, non ad Cretam iter facere voluisse. hoc <u>somnio</u>
   ceteris nuntiato, postridie multis cum lacrimis domos et Cretam reliquerunt.

Based on Virgil, Aeneid III.1-191.

Vocabulary

ora, orae (f)	shore
moenia, moenium (n pl)	walls
pestilentia, pestilentiae (f)	plague
somnium, somnii (n)	dream

(a) In line 1, how long did the journey to Crete take? [1]

(b) Lines 2-3:
  (i) what did the Trojans do when they reached Crete? [2]
  (ii) pick out **two** Latin words or phrases which tell us that the Trojans
  quickly set to work. You do not need to translate. [2]
  (iii) in these lines, three types of construction **inside** the city are
  described. What were they, and how complete were they? [3]

(c) What did the plague do? [3]

(d) **(i)** In lines 5-6, how did Aeneas learn the cause of the plague? Give full
  details. [3]
  (ii) What was the cause of the plague? [1]

(e) In line 7, what mistake did Aeneas learn that he had made? [2]

(f) What happened after Aeneas learnt the truth? [3]

[20]

Total [60]

XVII. *AENEAS SEEKS A NEW HOME II*

1 Read the first section of the story carefully, then answer all the questions.

*The Trojans, on their way to Italy, were driven by a storm sent by
the goddess Juno to the coast of Africa, where Aeneas' mother,
Venus, appeared to him.*

1 <u>Aeneas</u> <u>Troianos</u> trans mare ducebat. novam domum in <u>Italia</u> quaerebant.
2 <u>Iuno</u> autem, quod <u>Troianos</u> oderat, eos ad <u>Italiam</u> advenire nolebat.
3 tempestatem igitur tam gravem sustulit, ut omnes naves ad <u>Africam</u>
4 ferrentur. <u>Troiani</u>, paene confecti, vix naves ad terram duxerunt. ubi
5 <u>Aeneas</u> ad summum <u>collem</u> ascendit ut locum inspiceret, dea <u>Venus</u>, quae
mater eius erat, subito apparuit, <u>formam</u> vultumque puellae gerens.

Names

Aeneas, Aeneae (m) (accusative *Aenean*)	Aeneas
Troiani, Troianorum (m pl)	Trojans
Italia, Italiae (f)	Italy
Iuno, Iunonis (f)	Juno
Africa, Africae (f)	Africa
Venus, Veneris (f)	Venus

Vocabulary

collis, collis (m)	hill
forma, formae (f)	shape, appearance

(a) In line 1, what was Aeneas doing? [1]
(b) In line 1, what were the Trojans seeking? [1]
(c) *Iuno...nolebat* (line 2): what was Juno's attitude towards the Trojans? [2]
(d) *tempestatem...ferrentur* (lines 3-4): what happened to the Trojans? [2]
(e) In line 4, how are the Trojans described? [1]
(f) In line 5, what did Aeneas do, and why? [2]
(g) What was unusual about Venus' sudden appearance? [1]

[10]

XVII. *AENEAS SEEKS A NEW HOME II*

2 Read this section carefully and then translate it into English. **Please write your translation on alternate lines.**

> *Venus told Aeneas that Dido was the ruler of Carthage and would welcome the Trojans. Aeneas was upset by his mother's disguise.*

Venus 'haec terra' inquit 'Carthago est, cuius regina est Dido. in urbem suam Dido libenter vos accipiet. regina enim maritum non habet, quod frater eum necavit. fratrem magnopere timet.' tum dea Aenean rogavit, quis esset et unde venisset. Aeneas respondit se Troianum esse. 'dei' inquit 'nobis non favent.' 'sed ego vobis faveo' dea dixit. his verbis dictis, statim abiit. Aeneas, qui matrem iam agnovit, voce eam secutus est: 'nimis crudelis es, mater. cur me sic decipis? cur mihi dextram non das?' cum Aeneas ad suos tristis rediisset, nuntiavit quid accidisset. navibus prope mare relictis, profecti sunt ut urbem Didonis peterent.

Names

Carthago, Carthaginis (f)	Carthage
Dido, Didonis (f)	Dido

Vocabulary

agnosco, agnoscere, agnovi, agnitus	I recognise
nimis	too
decipio, decipere, decepi, deceptus	I deceive
dextra, dextrae (f)	right hand

[30]

3 Read this final section of the story carefully, then answer all the questions.

Aeneas went to inspect the city of Carthage.

1 Troiani, postquam montem transierunt, urbem conspexerunt; quae tanta ac
2 tam pulchra erat ut omnes eam <u>mirarentur</u>. in omnibus partibus novae urbis
3 erat <u>multitudo</u> hominum diligenter laborantium, nam cives omnia conficere
4 conabantur: alii muros, alii vias, alii forum parabant. maximum aedificium
5 erat templum Iunonis; ceteris viris <u>extra</u> urbem relictis, Aeneas ad hoc
   templum venit. quamquam non confectum erat, iam mirabile erat. cum
7 intravisset, Aeneas <u>picturas</u> in muris conspexit, in quibus quidam bellum
   Troianum <u>pinxerat</u>. ubi tot comites ibi fortiter pugnantes sed qui iam
   mortui erant vidit, lacrimavit. credidit autem reginam sibi auxilium
   daturam esse.

Based on Virgil, Aeneid I.

Vocabulary

miror, mirari, miratus sum	I admire
multitudo, multitudinis (f)	multitude
extra + acc.	outside
pictura, picturae (f)	picture, painting
pingo, pingere, pinxi, pictus	I paint

(a) In line 1, what did the Trojans do before seeing the city? [1]

(b) *quae…mirarentur* (lines 1-2): describe the city and its effect on the Trojans. [3]

(c) *in omnibus…laborantium* (lines 2-3): write down three things the Trojans saw in the city that indicated extensive activity. [3]

(d) In line 4, **three** types of construction work are mentioned. What are they? [3]

(e) **(i)** In line 5, which building is mentioned? [1]
    (ii) What was special about it? [1]

(f) What did Aeneas do before approaching this building? [2]

(g) *picturas* (line 7):
    (i) what did Aeneas see in these? [1]
    (ii) why did they make Aeneas cry? [3]

(h) Explain how the *picturae*, besides making Aeneas cry, also gave him hope. [2]

[20]

Total [60]

XVIII. *PIRATES I*

1 Read the first section of the story carefully, then answer all the questions.

*Julius Caesar had to flee for his life when he
asked for too much.*

Iulius Caesar, ubi iuvenis erat, sacerdos esse cupiebat. quod eo tempore
Sulla maximum imperium Romae tenebat, Caesar ad eum adiit. 'si me
sacerdotem facies' inquit 'gratias tibi agam.' sed illi hoc non placuit;
credidit enim Caesarem nimis iuvenem esse. ubi Caesar hunc honorem
iterum petivit, Sulla in animo habuit eum occidere. quo cognito Caesar
Roma celeriter fugit priusquam necaretur.

Names

Iulius Caesar, Iulii Caesaris (m)   Julius Caesar
Sulla, Sullae (m)   Sulla (dictator of Rome)

Vocabulary

nimis   too (much)

(a)	In the first sentence, what did Julius Caesar want?	[1]
(b)	Why did Caesar go to Sulla?	[2]
(c)	What did Caesar say to Sulla?	[2]
(d)	Why did Sulla refuse?	[2]
(e)	How did Sulla react when Caesar asked again?	[2]
(f)	What did Caesar do to save himself?	[1]

[10]

2 Read this section carefully and then translate it into English. **Please write your translation on alternate lines.**

Captured by pirates, Caesar made fun of them.

Caesar ab urbe effugiebat. trans mare cum paucis amicis in parva nave navigabat. piratae quidam, quorum eo tempore multi erant in omnibus maris partibus, eos captos ad parvam insulam duxerunt; hic Caesarem captivum tenebant. pretio viginti talentorum pro vita sua petito, Caesar risit. clamavit eos nescire quem cepissent. promisit se eis quinquaginta talenta daturum esse. amicos suos Romam misit ad hanc pecuniam quaerendam. dum eos exspectat, conabatur piratis imperare ut facerent id quod ipse volebat. etiam carmina et orationes quas scripserat recitabat, ac nisi plauserunt, eos stultissimos appellabat. cum saepe clamavisset se eos necaturum esse, credebant haec verba inania esse.

Vocabulary

pirata, piratae (m)	pirate
viginti	twenty
talentum, talenti (n)	talent (a gold coin)
quinquaginta	fifty
oratio, orationis (f)	speech
recito, recitare, recitavi, recitatus	I recite
plaudo, plaudere, plausi, plausus	I applaud
appello, appellare, appellavi, appellatus	I call
inanis, inane	empty, meaningless

[30]

XVIII. *PIRATES I*

3 Read this final section of the story carefully, then answer all the questions.

Caesar got his revenge on the pirates.

simulatque amici redierunt, pretium promissum ferentes, Caesar liberatus
naves quaerere coepit. quibus navibus ad insulam, in qua captivus fuerat,
3 regressus, piratas oppugnatos facile cepit. non solum quinquaginta talenta,
4 quae ipse eis tradiderat, recepit, sed etiam omnia quae habebant sibi rapuit.
5 homines ipsos ad proximam urbem ad <u>carcerem</u> in navibus transportavit.
tum ad <u>procuratorem</u> ivit, quem rogaret ut piratas puniret; cum tamen
7 intellexisset illum pecuniam, non homines cupere, ipse ad <u>carcerem</u>
8 festinavit, priusquam <u>procurator</u> milites mitteret ad pecuniam rapiendam;
piratas extractos omnes interfecit, sicut eis promiserat. deinde abiit, multo
divitior quam antea.

Based on Plutarch, Life of Caesar.

Vocabulary

carcer, carceris (m)	prison
procurator, procuratoris (m)	governor, chief magistrate

(a) How did Caesar win his freedom?   [2]
(b) How did Caesar use the ships?   [2]
(c) *piratas...cepit* (line 3): what **two** things did Caesar do to the pirates?   [2]
(d) *non solum...rapuit* (lines 3-4): how did Caesar profit from his actions?   [4]
(e) *homines...transportavit* (line 5): what happened to the pirates?   [2]
(f) **(i)** How did Caesar plan to punish the pirates?   [1]
     (ii) Why did this plan not work?   [3]
(g) *ipse...rapiendam* (lines 7-8): when Caesar hurried to the prison, what
was he anxious to avoid?   [2]
(h) Describe how Caesar gained full revenge on the pirates.   [2]

[20]

Total [60]

XIX. *PIRATES II*

1 Read the first section of the story carefully, then answer all the questions.

The pirates became very successful.

1 multi <u>piratae</u> iam erant in omnibus partibus maris. dum enim legiones
2 Romanae contra alios hostes pugnant, <u>piratae</u> tam audaces erant ut non
3 solum naves sed etiam insulas urbesque oppugnarent. ita brevi tempore
4 divitissimi facti sunt. erant inter <u>piratas</u> etiam viri nobiles, qui credebant
5 magnum honorem esse in tali vita. multos portus, in quibus tuti erant,
6 habebant. naves eorum celerrimae erant.

Vocabulary

pirata, piratae (m)   pirate

(a) In the first sentence, where were the pirates?   [2]
(b) In lines 1-2, what made the pirates bold?   [2]
(c) What did the pirates' boldness lead them to do?   [2]
(d) *ita…facti sunt* (lines 3-4): what was the result of their actions?   [1]
(e) Why did some noblemen join the pirates?   [1]
(f) *multos…erant* (lines 5-6): give **two** reasons for the pirates' success. [2]

[10]

XIX. *PIRATES II*

2 Read this section carefully and then translate it into English. **Please write your translation on alternate lines.**

> *The pirates were such a menace, especially to Roman citizens,*
> *that Rome was finally forced to send Pompey against them*
> *with huge forces at his disposal.*

pessimum scelus piratarum erat magistratus aut cives divites abripere, tum pecuniam pro eis postulare. ei captivi, qui clamaverunt se cives Romanos esse, necati sunt, nisi promiserunt suos plurimam pecuniam piratis daturos esse. mox mare tam plenum piratarum fuit ut nemo navigare vellet; Romae igitur populus frumentum non accepit. tandem senatores Pompeium emiserunt ad piratas opprimendos; cui imperium terra marique datum est. naves quoque quingentas, et viginti quattuor legiones accepit. Pompeius cum omnibus his copiis Roma profectus est. mari in tredecim partes diviso, duces Romani piratas in omnibus partibus simul oppugnaverunt; ita illi circumdati captique sunt. mox totum mare liberum fuit.

Names

Pompeius, Pompeii (m)	Pompey

Vocabulary

scelus, sceleris (n)	crime
magistratus, magistratus (m)	public official
aut	or
quingenti, quingentae, quingenta	five hundred
viginti	twenty
copiae, copiarum (f pl)	forces
tredecim	thirteen
divido, dividere, divisi, divisus	I divide
simul	simultaneously
circumdo, circumdare, circumdedi,	
circumdatus	I surround
liber, libera, liberum	free

[30]

3 Read this final section of the story carefully, then answer all the questions.

Pompey received a warm welcome in Rome, but had to leave
once more to deal with those pirates who had survived.

1 piratis victis Pompeius Romam rediit. plurimi cives ad portas convenerunt
2 ut eum in urbem ingredientem salutarent. cives enim gaudebant quod
3 tabernae iam plenae erant omnium rerum. pauci tamen piratae, qui non
4 occisi erant, in <u>Ciliciam</u> effugerant; nam hic castra in montibus habebant.
   Pompeius, simulac hoc cognovit, timebat ne piratae nautas <u>vectores</u>que
6 iterum <u>vexare</u> conarentur. Roma igitur profectus piratas tam celeriter
7 secutus est ut brevissimo tempore alios in <u>proelio</u> interficeret, alios caperet.
8 quorum pessimis in <u>carcerem</u> missis, ceteros, castris deletis, liberavit. hoc
9 bellum tribus <u>mensibus</u> confectum est.

Based on Plutarch, Life of Pompey.

Names

Cilicia, Ciliciae (f)   Cilicia (a Roman province in
                                         Asia)

Vocabulary

vector, vectoris (m)   traveller, sea-farer
vexo, vexare, vexavi, vexatus   I trouble
proelium, proelii (n)   battle
carcer, carceris (m)   prison
mensis, mensis (m)   month

(a) What did Pompey do after defeating the pirates?   [1]
(b) *plurimi…salutarent* (lines 1-2): describe Pompey's reception.   [3]
(c) What made the citizens happy?   [2]
(d) *pauci…habebant* (lines 3-4): explain what was happening in Cilicia. [4]
(e) Why did Pompey react to these events?   [2]
(f) *Roma…caperet* (lines 6-7): write down and translate **two** words or
         phrases that emphasise the speed with which Pompey dealt with the   [4]
         pirates.
(g) *quorum…liberavit* (line 8): explain what happened to the two groups of
         pirates.   [3]
(h) *hoc bellum…confectum est* (lines 8-9): what information are we given
         about the war?   [1]

[20]

Total [60]

XX. *CIPUS*

1 Read the first section of the story carefully, then answer all the questions.

The victorious general, Cipus, surprised to find himself growing horns, prayed to the gods.

1 <u>Cipus</u> erat imperator Romanus. olim, postquam hostes in <u>proelio</u> prope
2 flumen vicit, se in aqua fluminis forte conspexit. <u>attonitus</u> erat ubi <u>cornua</u>
3 in summo capite vidit. quod hoc signum verum esse non credidit, manus ad
4 caput sustulit: ea quae viderat <u>tetigit</u>. tum manibus oculisque ad caelum
5 sublatis, 'o di' inquit 'facite, oro, hoc signum laetum et mihi et populo
6 Romano.'

Names

Cipus, Cipi (m)   Cipus

Vocabulary

proelium, proelii (n)	battle
attonitus, attonita, attonitum	astonished
cornu, cornus (n)	horn
tango, tangere, tetigi, tactus	I touch

(a) In the first sentence, what information are we given about Cipus? [1]
(b) *olim...vicit* (lines 1-2): describe the success that Cipus had had. [2]
(c) In line 2, what did Cipus chance to do? [1]
(d) What surprised Cipus? [2]
(e) *manus ad caput sustulit* (lines 3-4): why did Cipus do this? [2]
(f) In lines 5-6, what prayer did Cipus make? [2]

[10]

2   Read this section carefully and then translate it into English. **Please write your translation on alternate lines.**

> *Cipus' horns were interpreted as a sign that he would be*
> *king of Rome. Cipus tried to avoid this fate.*

Cipus aram deis prope urbem Romam posuit. ibi vinum fudit <u>victima</u>sque
necavit. ubi sacerdos <u>exta</u> inspexit, signa magnarum rerum vidit. deinde
oculis ad cornua in capite Cipi sublatis, 'salve, o rex' inquit. 'tibi enim
tuisque cornibus omnes cives huius loci libenter parebunt. nunc in urbem
rursus festina. nam in urbem acceptus rex eris.' Cipus autem, his verbis
territus, ad urbem appropinquare noluit. deos oravit ne talia <u>permitterent</u>:
maluit enim in <u>exsilium</u> ire quam rex esse, quod, sicut plurimi Romani,
omnes reges malos esse credebat. statim populo ac senatoribus <u>extra</u> muros
Romae convocatis, cornibusque celatis, rem tam malam avertere conatus
est.

Vocabulary

victima, victimae (f)	victim (for sacrifice)
exta, extorum (n pl)	entrails, insides
permitto, permittere, permisi, permissus	I permit
exsilium, exsilii (n)	exile
extra + acc.	outside

[30]

XX. *CIPUS*

3 Read this final section of the story carefully, then answer all the questions.

*The Romans, persuaded not to let Cipus enter Rome,
yet honoured him with land.*

1 'adest quidam' inquit Cipus 'qui, nisi vos eum <u>expuleritis</u>, rex erit. nomen
2 eius non dicam, sed signum vobis dabo: cornua in capite gerit! sacerdos
3 dixit eum, Romam ingressum, regem futurum esse. quamquam portae urbis
4 apertae sunt, ille non intravit. ego enim ei restiti.' sic Cipus civibus
5 persuadere conatus est ne talem hominem in urbem acciperent. omnes
6 autem cognoscere voluerunt quis esset homo; capita inspicere coeperunt.
7 tum Cipus sua cornua ostendit; omnes, oculis in caput eius versis, rem
   intellexerunt. senatores, quod eum in urbem accipere non ausi sunt,
   maximum <u>praedium</u> prope urbem ei dederunt.

Based on Ovid, Metamorphoses XV.565-619.

Vocabulary

expello, expellere, expuli, expulsus	I drive out, expel
praedium, praedii (n)	estate

(a) In line 1, what warning did Cipus give the Romans? [3]
(b) *signum vobis dabo* (line 2): what did this *signum* consist of? [1]
(c) Explain how the information Cipus gave in line 3 relates to the warning
 he gave in line 1. [3]
(d) *quamquam...restiti* (lines 3-4):
 (i) why would it have been easy for the man Cipus was describing to
 enter the city? [1]
 (ii) what prevented this man from entering? [1]
(e) In his speech, Cipus was deceiving the Romans. What was the nature
 of this deception, and what was its purpose? [2+2]
(f) In lines 5-6, in what **two** ways did the Romans react to Cipus' speech? [3]
(g) *Cipus sua cornua ostendit* (line 7): what effect did this action have? [1]
(h) Explain how and why Cipus gained from this episode. [3]

[20]

Total [60]

Mark Schemes

Notes on using the mark schemes

1. Sections 1 and 3

The answers given in the mark schemes are only specimen answers: wording may vary substantially from that given; what matters is that the thought behind the Latin words be correctly rendered.

Since half-marks are no longer allowed to be used in the examination, they have been replaced by a doubling of the raw marks. This is to avoid as far as possible the need for two or more Latin words to be translated in order to gain one mark. When you have marked each of these two sections, you should halve your total, rounding up a half mark the first time, and rounding it down the second time.

2. Section 2

In the examination, each Latin word (unless a simple name or a glossed or repeated word) is allocated 1, 2 or (rarely) 3 marks according to its difficulty. Uninflected words usually carry 1 mark for the meaning. Where 2 marks are allocated, 1 will be for meaning, and 1 for ending (i.e. syntactical relationship). Where 3 marks are allocated (usually complex verbs or superlatives), 1 will be for meaning, 1 for tense, and 1 for voice or mood; or 1 for meaning, one for superlative, and one for agreement. In this book, these marks are shown over the translation instead of the Latin, but the principle is identical. Italics indicate where a word or part of a word carries no mark. When marking the translation, remember to deduct two marks if you have got both meaning and ending wrong, but award yourself one mark if you get one of these elements correct.

Because there are rarely enough raw marks available to treat every word the same in a passage of Latin, you will find that many verbs carry only one mark, which means that both the meaning and the ending must be correctly rendered to gain the mark.

This method is precise but laborious. There are two alternatives you can use to save time:

(a) *negative marking*: this is for translations which are on the whole accurate. Here each mistake is underlined and the mark relating to the error deducted from the total for that sub-section. Care must be taken that the correct number of marks is deducted for each word: thus, if a word carrying two marks is wrong in both meaning and syntax, it will be underlined twice and lose both marks; if, however, its meaning is wrong but its syntax right, it will be underlined once and lose only one of its marks. If applied carefully, this method should give results as precise as the first method.

71

(b) *rough percentage*: since each Section 2 passage contains exactly 100 words, you can simply award yourself one mark for every Latin word you have translated correctly; you will end up with a percentage rather than a mark out of 30, but you can easily convert the total if you wish. This method is quick and not as accurate, but will give you an approximation of your standard.

As with Sections 1 and 3, the specimen translation is only a guide to the meaning; it is the sense, not the constructions, that is being marked. Thus a change from active to passive is quite acceptable provided that the agent is expressed. There are many acceptable ways of translating an ablative absolute phrase into English: for example, *hoc dicto abiit* may be translated as 'this said (s)he went away', '(s)he said this and went away', 'having said this, (s)he went away' and so on. You will need to exercise your judgement when deciding whether your version adequately renders the meaning or not.

I. *MIDAS*

1

(a) king (1) of Phrygia (1) [2]
(b) a few (1) Phrygians (1) captured him (1) drunk (1) in (1) the woods (1) [6]
(c) he was (1) old (1) he was a friend (1) of Bacchus (1) [4]
(d) they led / took him (1) to the king / Midas (1) [2]
(e) he was (1) happy (1) when (1) he recognised (1) who (1) he was (1) [6]
(f) for ten (1) days (1) and nights (1) he gave (1) a feast (1) to (all) the citizens (1) [6]
(g) he gave (1) back (1) / restored (2) Silenus / the old man (1) to Bacchus (1) [4]

[30 / 2 = 15]

2

   1 1   1   1   1 1   1   1 1 1   1
His friend having been given_back / restored, the god promised to give *Midas*
1 1   **14**
a gift.
1 1   1   1   1   1 1 1 1   1   **10**
'I shall give you *whatever* you wish,' he said.
  11 1   1 1   1 1 1   1   1 1 1   **12**
'Turn to *gold* everything (which) I *touch*,' *Midas* replied to the god.
   1   1 11 11   1   1 1 1 1   **11**
Although the god was sad because *Midas was* so foolish,
1 1 1   1   1 1 1   1   **8**
he *gave* him the *gift* which he had asked for.
1 1   1   1   1 1   **6**
The king went away / left rejoicing / happy.
1 1 1   1   1   1   1   1   1   **9**
He pulled a *branch* from a *tree*: at once the *branch* was made *of gold*.

```
 1   1      1    1 1 1  1     1          1   1                      10
```
When he *touch*ed the door of his house, the *door* also *was made of gold.*
```
 1   1      1  1      1  1 1 1  1  1                                 10
```
Even the water in(to) which he placed his hand *was made of gold.*
```
 1          1   1 1         1   1  1  1  1  1                        10
```
So / thus the *king* hoped to be / that he would be very *rich* soon.

Total: 100. Divide this total by 4 to reach final mark out of 25.   **[25]**

3
(a) placed / set (1) a dinner / meal (1) for (1) the king (1)   [4]
(b) he brought (1) bread (1) to his mouth (1) the bread (1) was (1) hard (1) he
   wanted (1) to drink (1) wine (1) from (1) a golden (1) cup (1) when (1)
   the wine (1) touched (1) his mouth (1) it was made (1) of gold (1)   [18]
(c) how (1) foolish (1) he had (1) been (1)   [4]
(d) he raised (1) (his) shining (1) arms (1) to the sky (1) and prayed (1) to the
   god (1) to spare (1) him (1)   [8]
(e) because (1) he was (1) kind (1) Bacchus (1) saved (1) the king / Midas (1) [6]
                                                               [40 / 2 = 20]
                                                      Total for *Midas* [60]

II. *PICUS AND CANENS*

1
(a) king (1) of Ausonia (1)   [2]
(b) **(i)** he was (1) handsome / beautiful (1)   [2]
   (ii) many (1) girls (1) who lived (1) in Ausonia (1) loved (1) him (1)   [6]
(c) a crowd (1) of girls (1) came (1) to his house (1) to watch / see (1)
   him (1)   [6]
(d) he rejected (2) all (1) the girls (1) except (1) one (1)   [6]
(e) **(i)** she was (1) more beautiful (1) than (1) (all) the rest (1) she sang (1)
   sweetly (1)   [6]
   (ii) she was called (1) 'Canens' (1)   [2]
                                                               [30 / 2 = 15]

2
```
 1     1  11  1 1              1  1 1            1  1     1  1        13
```
Once *Picus* left home / his house to seek / look for *boars* in the woods.
```
 1   1  1 1    1  1     1    1     1  1     1 1                       12
```
Circe, who was a dreadful *witch*, was walking in the same *woods.*
```
 1   1  1 1    1   1  1  1          1                                9
```
When she saw *Picus*, she desired / wanted him.
```
 1        1 1  1   1      1    1        1  1                         9
```
Because (his) horse was quickly carrying *Picus* away_from her,

```
1    1  1  1 1              1      1                                    7
```
she *could* not catch / capture him at once.
```
1       1    11     11    1 1          1                                9
```
She therefore sent a huge *boar* to(wards) him.
```
1      1 1             1    1 1  1    1     1  11 1                    12
```
Picus, when he *saw* / had seen the *boar*, wanted to capture and kill it.
```
1     1       1          1  1 1     1        1                          8
```
He *jumped down* from *his horse* and hurried through the *woods*.
```
1  1 1     1      1 1                                                   6
```
Soon he was *far* from his friends.
```
1     1   1 1        1   1  1 1 1 1  1 1      1 1      1               15
```
Suddenly *Circe* stood *before* him, who asked him to accept *and* return *her love*.

Total: 100. Divide this total by 4 to reach final mark out of 25.   **[25]**

3

(a) whoever (1) you are (1) I am not (1) yours (1) I love (1) another (1) and
always (1) shall love her (1)   [8]

(b) she was (1) angry (1) you will be (1) punished (1) she said (1) if (1) you
reject (1) me (1) you will (1) never (1) return (1) to Canens (1)   [12]

(c) he ran away / fled (2) very (1) quickly (1) but (1) could (1) not (1) escape (1) [8]

(d) when (1) he had not (1) returned (1) home (1)   [4]

(e) she searched for (1) him (1) for many (1) days (1)   [4]

(f) *frustra* (2) in vain (2) / *exspiravit* (2) she died (2)   [4]

                                                          [40 / 2 = 20]

                                        Total for *Picus and Canens* [60]

III. *DAEDALUS AND ICARUS*

1

(a) he was (1) a craftsman (1) he lived (1) in the island (1) of Crete (1)
for (1) many (1) years (1)   [8]

(b) to return (1) to Athens (1) he was born (1) there (1)   [4]

(c) the king (1) ordered him (1) to stay (1) there / in Crete (1)   [4]

(d) the king (1) controls / rules (1) the land (1) and (1) the sea (1) but /
though (1) not (1) the sky (1)   [8]

(e) he put (1) feathers (1) long (1) and short (1) on the ground (1) he
bound (1) them (1) (together) with wax (1) (Accept any six points.)   [6]

                                                          [30 / 2 = 15]

2

```
1         1 1    1  1            1         1  1 1  1 1 1              12
```
*Daedalus complete*d the wings for_himself; the *wings* were excellent / very good.

| | | | | |
1　　　　　1　 1 1　　　　　1　1　　11　　1　1　　　1　　　　**11**
When *the wings were* ready, the craftsman threw himself into the sky,
11　　　　11　 1　　　　　　　　　　　　　　　**5**
*lift*ing up his body on /by the *wings*.
　1　1　　1　1　　1　　　1　 1 1　1　　1　　　**10**
When he understood that the *wings* carried him easily,
1　1　1　11　　1　　　　　　　1　　1　　1　　**9**
he made other *wings* / a second set of wings for his son, named *Icarus*.
1　1　　1　1　1　　1　　　　1　　　　　**7**
For he did not want to escape *without* his *son*.
1　　1　1　　　1　　　　　　　**4**
With these also *complete*d / When these were also completed,
1　1 1　 1 1 1 11　 1 1　　1　　　**11**
he warned the boy to hold a middle *course*:
1　1　　1　　1　 1 1　1　1　1　　　1　 1 1　**12**
'If you *fly* near the sea,' he said, 'the waves will *make* the *wings* heavy,
　1　1　　　1　　　　　　　**3**
and you will *fall (down)* into *the sea*;
1　　　　1　　1　1　1　　1　1　　**7**
if however *you fly near* the *sun*, the *heat* will burn the feathers.
　1　1　1　 11　1 1　1　1　　**9**
If you fly near me, there will *be* no danger for you.'

Total: 100. Divide this total by 4 to reach final mark out of 25.　　**|25|**

3
(a) father (1) and son (1) raised (1) themselves (1) / rose (2) into (1)
　　　the sky (1)　　　**[6]**
(b) many (1) hours (1)　　　**[2]**
(c) he began (1) to fly (1) higher (2) delighted (1) by (1) the new (1)
　　　wings (1)　　　**[8]**
(d) the sun (1) melted / made soft (1) the wax (1) all (1) the feathers (1)
　　　fell (1) into (1) the sea (1)　　　**[8]**
(e) he also (1) fell (1)　　　**[2]**
(f) **(i)** (when) he looked (1) back (1)　　　**[2]**
　　　(ii) he looked for (2) him (1) far and wide / widely (1) he saw (1) the
　　　wings (1) among (1) the waves (1)　　　**[8]**
(g) it was (1) recovered / taken back (1) (and) placed (1) in a tomb (1) /
　　　buried (2)　　　**[4]**
　　　　　　　|40 / 2 = 20|
　　　Total for *Daedalus and Icarus* |60|

IV. *CEPHALUS AND PROCRIS*

1

(a) he was (1) old (1)   [2]
(b) an island (2)   [2]
(c) he had not seen (1) them (1) for many (1) years (1)   [4]
(d) (he asked) about (1) the spear (1) which (1) he was carrying (1)   [4]
(e) the spear (1) was strange / wonderful (1)   [2]
(f) **(i)** he cried (2) always (2)   [4]
       (ii) it brought / caused (1) death (1) to (1) his wife (1)   [4]
(g) her name (1) was Procris (1) (she was) very (1) beautiful (1) (she was)
       very (1) sweet (1) he loved her (1) very much (1)   [8]
                                                                            [30 / 2 = 15]

2

    1   1 1 1   1 1 1   11 11 1   1   **13**
Cephalus was telling / told the story of / about his life to his friends.
   1   1 1   1 1   1 1 1 1 1 1 1 1   1
'Once,' he said, 'the goddess *Aurora* saw me and took me away, because
   1 1 1   **17**
she loved me:
 1   1 1   1   1   1   1   1 1   **9**
But I did not wish / refused to *love* her, *because* I *prefer*red my wife.
 1 1 1   1   1 1 1   1   **8**
Angry she at last returned me / gave me back to *my wife*.
  1   1 1   1   1 1 1 1   **8**
but she promised that we would be unhappy.
   1 1   1   1 1   1 1 1   **8**
While I was walking home, I *began* to fear / be afraid:
1 1   1   1 1 1 1   **7**
was *Procris* even then faithful?
  1   1 1   1   1 1 1   1 1 1
*Aurora change*d my *appearance*, so that I could / might watch and *secretly*
 1   1   **12**
test Procris.
 1 1 1 1 1 1   1 1 1   1   1 1 1   **13**
Procris, who did not know me, (at) first did not *wish* to accept my *love*;
    1   1   1   1 1   **5**
but at last she *hesitate*d. At once I *condemn*ed her.'

Total: 100. Divide this total by 4 to reach final mark out of 25.   [25]

3

(a) immediately (1) she fled (1) from (1) the house / home (1) (in)to (1) the
mountains (1) (where) she worshipped (1) Diana (1) [8]
(b) he found (1) her (1) he begged (1) her (1) to forgive (1) him (1) [6]
(c) she returned (1) home (1) with (1) him (1) for many (1) years (1) they
were very (1) happy (1) [8]
(d) **(i)** for (1) hunting (1) [2]
    (ii) the goddess (1) had given (1) it (1) to her (1) [4]
(e) that Procris (1) was going (1) after / behind (1) him (1) [4]
(f) Cephalus (1) saw (1) something (1) moving (1) he threw (1) his spear (1)
(the spear) killed (1) Procris (1) [8]

|40 / 2 = 20|

Total for *Cephalus and Procris* |60|

V. *NERO AND AGRIPPINA*

1

(a) **(i)** he loved (1) her (1) very (1) much (1) [4]
    (ii) she hated (1) her (1) [2]
(b) to kill (1) his mother (1) [2]
(c) how (1) he could (1) kill (1) her (1) [4]
(d) **(i)** he liked (1) it (1) [2]
    (ii) it was (1) difficult (1) to give her (1) poison (1) without her (1)
knowing (1) [6]
(e) thought of / thought up / came up with / took up / had / conceived /
suggested (or a similar word that naturally accompanies 'plan' or 'idea') [2]
(f) to build (1) a ship (1) when Agrippina (1) is in it (1) the roof (1)
will fall (1) on her (1) killing her (1) [8]

|30 / 2 = 15|

2

1   1   1 1   1   1   1 1   1   1   **10**
Anicetus persuaded / was persuading *Nero* that a ship be built.
   1 1 11   1   1   1   1 1   **9**
'The sea is always dangerous,' he said.
1   1   11 1   1 1   1   1   **9**
'if *Agrippina dies* in *the sea*, no one will *blame* you.'
   1 1 1   1 1   1   **6**
This plan pleased *Nero*.
   1   1   1   1 1   1 1 1   1 1 1   1 1   **14**
When the *ship* was prepared / ready, *Nero* invited his mother to *Baiae* to his
   1
house.

```
 1  1 1      1   1   1   1              1                  1                    1          10
```
He sent the *ship* to transport / carry her across through / during the night.
```
        1    11  1          1   11     1                                        8
```
Agrippina sat in the *ship* with two friends.

```
      1      1   1      1   1  1        1   1                                    8
```
When the *ship* had proceeded to the middle of *the sea*,
```
      1  1    1   1 1   1    1 1  1     1                                       10
```
a signal was given and the roof fell down.
```
 1 1  1           1          1      1      1                                     7
```
One of *Agrippina*'s *friends* was killed at once;
```
  1       1   1  1    1     1      1     1     1                                 9
```
she herself and the other *friend* were thrown into *the sea*.

Total: 100. Divide this total by 4 to reach final mark out of 25. [25]

3
(a) looked for (1) Agrippina (1) in (1) the water (1) [4]
(b) shouting / she shouted (2) she was (1) Agrippina (1) (and she) was (1)
       killed (1) [6]
(c) quietly (1) she swam (1) to shore (1) (and) so (1) reached (1) home (1) [6]
(d) (i) his mother (1) was (1) still (1) alive (1) [4]
     (ii) he was (2) very (1) angry (1) [4]
(e) he sent (1) three (1) soldiers (1) to (1) kill (1) her (1) [6]
(f) Agrippina was (1) terrified (1) she said (1) 'strike (1) my stomach /
       womb' (1) she was killed (1) with many (1) wounds (1) [8]
(g) It was the womb that had carried Nero (as a baby) / she wanted to appear
       brave / so that the wounds would not show (Give 1 mark for partial
       answer.) [2]
                                                          [40 / 2 = 20]
                                       Total for *Nero and Agrippina* [60]

VI. *APOLLO AND DAPHNE*

1
(a) daughter (1) of Peneus (1) very (1) beautiful (1) [4]
(b) many (1) sought her (1) she rejected (1) (them) all (1) [4]
(c) have (1) a husband (1) and (1) children (1) [4]
(d) she embraced (1) him (1) she (had) replied (1) 'I want to live (1) without
       a man / husband (1) without children' (1) (Accept indirect speech.) Any
       four points. [4]
(e) (i) the young men (1) pursued her there (1)
     (ii) she loved (1) to walk there (1) [4]
                                                          [20 / 2 = 10]

2

10

  1   1   1 1 1   1   1   1   1   1
Once *Apollo*, travelling through the woods, caught sight of *Cupid*.

4

  1 11   1
Cupid had *a bow*.

  1   1   1   1 1 1   1   1 1   1 1   1
Apollo, who was the best / a very good *archer*, ordered him to throw away *the*

12

bow:

10

 1   1   1   1   1 1   1   1 1   1
'You are not *an archer*,' he said, 'but a small boy.'

7

 1 1   1   1   1   11 1
Angry, *Cupid* at once shot / sent *an arrow* at / into *Apollo*,

10

  1   1   1   11 11 1   1   1
so that he would love the first girl (that) he saw.

7

 1 1   1   1   1   1   1
See! In the middle of the woods *Daphne* was walking!

8

    1   1 1   1   1   1   1   1
As soon as he saw her, *Apollo* was inflamed with love.

13

 1 1 1   1 1   1   1 1   1 11 1 1
He ran to her, already in his mind praising the *girl*'s face and *hair*.

10

 1   1   1 1   1   1   1   1 1
Cupid however *had* another / a second *arrow*, which would / to destroy *love*;

3

     1   1   1
he *shot* / *sent* this / it at / into *Daphne*.

10

 1   1   1   1   1   1   1   1   1 1
She therefore, when she saw / had seen the god approaching, fled.

6

   1   1   1   1   1   1
The more quickly *Apollo* followed, *the more quickly Daphne* ran away.

10

 1   1 1 1 1   1   1   1   1 1
He begged her to stop, but *the girl* refused / did not want to hear / listen.

Total: 120. Divide this total by 4 to reach final mark out of 30.   **[30]**

3

(a) a deer (1) fleeing (1) from (1) a lion (1)   [4]
(b) I am chasing (1) you (1) because (1) I love you (1) (Accept 3rd person.)   [4]
(c) **(i)**   she might (1) fall (down) (1) because the ground (1) is rough (1)   [4]
    (ii)   if she runs (1) more slowly (1) he will run (1) more slowly (1)   [4]
    (iii)   because then he would never catch her (or similar) (2)   [2]
(d) **(i)**   he said he was not (1) a poor farmer (1) but the son (1) of Jupiter (1)
    (Accept direct speech.)   [4]
    (ii)   none / she had gone (2)   [2]
(e) he ran (1) very quickly (1) motivated / moved (1) by love (1) she had
    begun (1) to stop (1)   almost (1) worn out (1)   [8]

(f)   she begged her father (1) to help (1)
      she called to him (1) to change her shape (1)
      as soon as (1) she said this (1) / at once (2)
      she became / was made (1) a tree (1)
      but Apollo still (1) loved her (1)
      (Accept any four pairs.)   **[8]**

[40 / 2 = 20]
Total for *Apollo and Daphne* [60]

VII. *CAMILLUS AT VEII*

1

(a)   waging war / fighting (1) against Veii (1) for ten (1) years (1)   **[4]**
(b)   he (had) promised (1) his men (1) a great (1) reward (1) he (had)
      asked (1) the gods (1) to give (him) (1) help (1)   **[8]**
(c)   to make / dig (1) a tunnel (1) under (1) the (city) walls (1)   **[4]**
(d)   some attacked (1) the walls (1) others hurried / ran (1) through the tunnel (1)   **[4]**

[20 / 2 = 10]

2

    1   1   1   1   1   1   1   1   1   **9**
Camillus was happy, because he had at last captured the city / town (of) Veii
1   1 1 1 1   1   **6**
and (had) killed many of the enemy.
      1   1 1 1   1   1   1   1   1 1   1
He *permit*ted his soldiers, to whom he had promised great rewards, to plunder
1   **12**
the *city*.
1 1   1   1   1   1   1 1   1   1   1   1   **13**
He sold for / at a *great* price those / the citizens of *Veii* who were still alive.
    1 1   1   1   1   1   1 1   **8**
He sent all the money received / accepted in this way / thus to *Rome*.
1   1 1   1   1   1   **6**
He also began to remove / carry away everything from_the_temples.
1   1   1 1   **4**
He even / also took / captured the *statue* of *Juno*.
1   1 1   1   1   **5**
But / however the band / group of young men,
1   1   1 1   1   1   1   **7**
who had been ordered to move the sacred *statue*,
1 1   1   1   1 1 1   **7**
feared that / lest the goddess might / would be angry.
1   1   1   1 1   1   **6**
One of the *young men* therefore addressed / spoke to the *goddess*:

　　1　　1　　　　　　　　1　　　1　1　　1　　　　　　1　1
'Do you wish / are you willing,' he said, 'queen of heaven / the sky, to go
　　1　1　　　　　　　　　　　　　　　　　　　　　　　　　　　10
with_us to *Rome?*'
　　　1　　1　1　　　　　　　1　　　　　　1　1　　　　　　　　6
The *statue* seemed / was seen to *nod* (with) its head.
　　1　　1　　1　　　　　　1　　　　　　　1　1　1　　　　　1　1
*Every*one believed / thought that the *goddess* wanted to see (her) *new* home /
house.　　　　　　　　　　　　　　　　　　　　　　　　　　　　9
　　1　　　1　　　1　　　1　　1　　　　1　1　　1　　　　　1　　　1 1
Although it was huge, it was easily transported to a new *temple* in *Rome*, built
1　　　　　　　　　　　　　　　　　　　　　　　　　　　　　　12
by *Camillus*.
Total: 120. Divide this total by 4 to reach final mark out of 30.　　**[30]**

3
(a) **(i)**　Veii (1) had been / was captured (1) after so many (1) years (1)　[4]
　　　(ii)　the citizens (1) rejoiced / were happy (1) the war was / had been (1)
　　　(so) long (1) (so) many soldiers (1) had been killed (1)　　　　[6]
(b)　they ran (1) to the temples (1) to thank (1) the gods (1)　　　　　[4]
(c) **(i)**　(it met / came to) greet (1) Camillus (1) entering (1) the city /
　　　town (1)　　　　　　　　　　　　　　　　　　　　　　　　[4]
　　　(ii)　they believed (1) he was (1) the greatest (1) of (all) commanders (1)　[4]
(d) **(i)**　he was carried / rode (1) into the city (1) in a splendid (1) chariot (1)　[4]
　　　(ii)　that he was rivalling (2) the gods (1) themselves (1) that he
　　　wanted (1) to make (1) himself (1) dictator (1)　　　　　　　[8]
(e)　he promised (1) two temples (1) he gave up (1) his power (1) because
　　　he'd done his job / carried out his orders / dues / what was owed / what
　　　he had to do (or similar) (2)　　　　　　　　　　　　　　[6]
　　　　　　　　　　　　　　　　　　　　　　　　　　　　[40 / 2 = 20]
　　　　　　　　　　　　　　　　　　　　Total for *Camillus at Veii* [60]

VIII. *CAMILLUS AT FALERII*

1
(a)　he was a Roman (1) commander / general (1) he (had) conquered (1)
　　　Veii (1)　　　　　　　　　　　　　　　　　　　　　　　[4]
(b)　they (had) helped (1) (the people of) Veii (1)　　　　　　　　[2]
(c)　Camillus would defeat (1) Falerii (1)　　　　　　　　　　　[2]
(d) **(i)**　he burned / began to burn (1) their (1) houses (1) and corn (1)　[4]
　　　(ii)　because the enemy (1) refused / did not wish (1) to leave (1)
　　　the city (1) / to make them (1) come out (1) to defend (1) these things (1)　[4]
(e)　as soon as (1) they emerged (1)
　　　they were (1) defeated (1)

many (1) were killed (1)
the rest fled (1) into the city (1)
(Accept any two pairs.) [4]
[20 / 2 = 10]

2

1 1 1 1 1 1		**6**

After the first *victory* against the citizens of *Falerii*,

1   1 1 1   1 1 1   1   1   **9**

the *Romans* began to *besiege* this city, just like *Veii*.

1   1   1   1   1 1   1

The *citizens* however after carrying much corn / much corn having been

1   1   **9**

carried into the city,

1   1   1 1   1   1   1   **6**

before all the roads / streets / ways were / might be / could be *blocked*,

1   1 1 1 1 1   1   1   1   **9**

had much more food even than the *Romans*.

1   1   1   1   1   1   **6**

Therefore they did not hand themselves over / surrender to the *Romans*.

1   1   1 1   1   1   1   1   **8**

And so / therefore *Camillus* believed / thought (that) he would capture the *city*

1   1   1 1   1   1   **6**

neither easily nor in a short time.

1   1   1   1   1   1   **6**

However / but in_the_*city* (there) was a (certain) *schoolmaster*;

1   1   1   1   1   **5**

because this *master* was very good / excellent / the best,

1 1   1   1 1   1   1 1   1   **9**

the boys, whom he taught, were the sons of nobles / noblemen / the nobility.

1   1 1 1   1   1   1

He was accustomed to lead(ing) / tak(ing) the *boys* out of / from_the_*city*

1   **8**

every day,

1   1   1 1   **4**

to *exercise* / so that they might exercise (their) bodies.

1   1 1   1   1   1   1 1   1

Although the war was being waged around_the_*city*, he did not fear the

1 1   **11**

enemy.

1   1   1   1 1   1 1   1

Once / one day he *led* / took the *boys* further from_the_*city* to the *Roman*(s')

1 1   **10**

camp.

82

    1   1   1   1 1   **8**
Having entered / (after) entering the *camp*, he went to / approached the
    1   1   1
commander himself.

Total: 120. Divide this total by 4 to reach final mark out of 30.   **[30]**

3
(a) what (1) he wanted (1) why (1) he had come (1)   [4]
(b) he had brought (1) to the Romans (1) all the noblemen's (1) sons (1) so
that they would have (1) hostages (1) (Accept direct speech.)   [6]
(c) if you hold / keep (1) them / these (as) hostages (1) you will soon
capture (1) Falerii (1) their fathers have (1) all the power (1) they will do
anything (1) to get them back (1) (Accept indirect speech.)   [8]
(d) the Romans did not do (1) such things (1)   [2]
(e) he gave the boys (1) sticks (1) to beat (1) the master (1)   [4]
(f) they were watching (2) from the walls (1) of the city (1)   [4]
(g) with how much / so much (1) honour (1) Camillus (1) acted (1)   [4]
(h) they believed / thought (1) they (would) prefer (1) Romans (1) so / such
just (1) to be (1) allies (1) rather than (1) enemies (1)   [8]
                                  [40 / 2 = 20]
                    Total for *Camillus at Falerii* [60]

IX. *PYRAMUS AND THISBE*

1
(a) (they lived) in neighbouring (1) houses (1)   [2]
(b) they were both (1) very beautiful (1)   [2]
(c) first they were (1) friends (1) then they loved (1) each other / fell in love (1)   [4]
(d) their fathers / mothers / parents (1) forbade (1) them (1) to meet (1)   [4]
(e) **(i)** it was small (1) it pierced (1) the wall (1) between the houses (1) it
was long (1) unseen / unknown (1)   [6]
    (ii) they could speak / communicate (1) through it (1)   [2]
                                [20 / 2 = 10]

2
          1   1 1   1   1   **5**
Pyramus and *Thisbe* talked *every day* through the crack.
  1   1 1 1   1   1   1 1 1   **9**
Often they said, 'O wall, why do you *stand in the way* of us lovers?
  1 1 1 1   1   1   1   1   1   1
When night was coming / came, having given *kisses* to the *wall*, they went
  1   1   **12**
away sad(ly).

1   1   1 1   1 1 1   1   1   1   **10**
Then, because they did not want to do the same things any longer,
1   1 1 1 1   1   1   1 1 1 1 1
they decided to go out of the houses *secretly* at *night and* meet at a certain
1   **14**
place:
1   1 1   1   1   1 1 1   **8**
this *place* was the *tomb of Ninius*, where there was a *tree* near a *spring*.
1   1 1 1   1 1   1 1   1 11   **11**
When *Thisbe*, setting out at the middle of the *night*, (had) reached the *tomb* first,
1 1 1   1 1 1   **6**
she sat under_the_*tree* to wait for *Pyramus*.
1 1 1 1 1 1 1   1 1   1   **10**
Suddenly a lion, whose face was *smeared* with blood,
1   1   1 1 11 1 1   **8**
approached the *spring* to drink water.
1   1 1 1   1 11 1   11 1 1   1 **13**
Thisbe, as soon as she saw the *lion*, fleeing into a *cave*, left her *veil* on the ground.
1 1 1   1 1 1   1   1 1 1 11   1 1   **14**
Seeing this the *lion tore* it *apart* so *violently* that he left much *blood on_it*.

Total: 120. Divide this total by 4 to reach final mark out of 30.   **[30]**

3
(a) the footprints (1) of the lion (1) the torn (1) veil (1)   **[4]**
(b) to die (1) he believed (1) Thisbe (1) was dead (1)   **[4]**
(c) he stabbed (1) himself (1) with his sword (1) his blood (1) poured (1) out
of the wound (1)   **[6]**
(d) she was afraid (1) she would not be there (1) when Pyramus (1) arrived (1) **[4]**
(e) she saw (1) his body (1) lying (1) on the ground (1)   **[4]**
(f) she embraced (1) Pyramus / her lover (1) she shed / poured tears /
wept (2) over / on top of (1) his wound (1)   **[6]**
(g) she recognised (1) the veil (1) she saw (1) the sword (1)   **[4]**
(h) **(i)**   to follow him (1) to death (1)   **[2]**
      (ii) 'if we shall not live (1) in the same house (1) we shall lie (1) in the
same tomb (1)   **[4]**
(i)   she fell (1) on the sword (1)   **[2]**
                             [40 / 2 = 20]
Total for *Pyramus and Thisbe* [60]

X. *GHOSTS*

1

(a) he was (1) noble (1) / he lived (1) in Africa (1) — [2]

(b) a female (1) figure (1) large (1) beautiful (1) — [4]

(c) *perterrito* (2) — [2]

(d) 'you will go (1) to Rome' (1) 'you will receive (1) honours' (1) 'you will return (1) to the province / Africa' (1) 'you will die (1) there' (1) (Accept indirect speech.) — [8]

(e) when he returned (1) to Africa (1) when he was getting off (1) the ship / boat (1) — [4]

[20 / 2 = 10]

2

1	1	1	1	1	5

At *Athens* (there) was a large but *disreputable* house;

  1 1   1   1   1 1 1 1 1 1 1   1   **12**

for in / through the *silence* of the night the sound of iron could be heard.

  1   1   1   1 1 1   1 1   1   1 1 **11**

Soon the *ghost* of an old man wearing / bearing *chains* on his hands appeared.

  1 1 1 1   1   1 1 1 1   1   1 **13**

Those who lived in the *house* spent / had such dreadful nights through fear

 1   1   1 1   1 1   1 1   **8**

that they never slept; death followed.

    1   1   1   1   1 1 1 1 1 1   **10**

Soon the *house* was *deserted*, because no one wanted to buy it.

  1   1   1 1   1 1   1

Then / afterwards *Athenodorus*, a *philosopher*, came to *Athens*, to *buy* a *house*

          1   **8**

for himself.

  1   1 1   1   1   1 1 1   1   1 1 **11**

Having seen this *house* and *hear*d the price, he handed over the money,

    1   1   1   1   1   1 1   **7**

although he had learnt / heard / he knew that there was a *ghost* there.

  1   1   1   1 1 1   1   1   1   1   1

When it was *night*, he ordered slaves to bring *writing tablets* into the first part

 1   **12**

of the *house*;

  1   1 1   1   **4**

there he began to write.

    1   1   1   1   1 1   **6**

(At) first (there) was *silence*; *then chains* were *heard* moving / being moved.

1   1   1 1 1   1 1   **7**

Athenodorus wrote / was writing, not raising *his* eyes.

1   1   1   1   1 1   **6**

Then the *sound* was *great*er / louder *and* nearer.

Total: 120. Divide this total by 4 to reach final mark out of 30.   **[30]**

3

(a) a ghost (1) as (1) had been (1) described (1) standing (1) by the door (1) signalling (1) with its hand (1)   **[8]**

(b) he was not (1) frightened (1) he ordered (1) the ghost (1) to wait (1) he (began to) write (again) (1)   **[6]**

(c) it approached (1) him (1) it shook chains (1) over his head (1)   **[4]**

(d) he got up (1) at last (1) from the couch (1) to follow (1) the ghost (1) into the garden (1)   **[6]**

(e) it was (1) old (1) / it was weighed down (1) by chains (1)   **[2]**

(f)   **(i)**   he ordered (1) his slaves (1) to dig up (1) the place (1)   **[4]**
      (ii) he believed (1) the body (1) of a man (1) lay there (1)   **[4]**

(g) bones (1) were found (1)
enclosed (1) in chains (1)
these were buried (1) by a priest (1)
this was what the ghost (1) had wanted (1)
(Accept any three pairs.)   **[6]**

[40 / 2 = 20]
Total for *Ghosts* [60]

XI. *DEIPHOBUS*

1

(a) leader (1) of the Trojans / Troy (1)   **[2]**

(b) to see (1) his father (1)   **[2]**

(c) walking (1) among the spirits (1)   **[2]**

(d) he had been (1) Aeneas' friend (1) many years (1) before (1)
he had been (1) killed (1) defending (1) Troy (1)   **[8]**

(e) he did not know (1) he was dead (1) his appearance (1) was dreadful (1)
he had neither nose (1) nor ears (1)   **[6]**

[20 / 2 = 10]

2

1   1 1   1   **4**

Aeneas approached / went to *Deiphobus.*

1 1 1   1   1   1   **6**

He asked him what had happened.

1   1   1 1 1 1   1 1 1   1   **10**
'In the city,' *Aeneas* said, 'I heard you (had) fought very bravely.
 1 1   1 1 1 1 1 1 1   **9**
I tried to find you, but could not.
     1 1 1   **3**
But who did this / these things?'
 1 1 1 1   1 1 1   1 1 1   **10**
He replied that *Aeneas could* not have done more.
   1   1   1   1   **4**
'It was *Helen*,' *he said*, 'who *did* this.'
 1 1 1   1   1 1 1   **7**
At that time *Helen* was the wife of *Deiphobus*,
  1 1   1   1   1 1   1 1 **10**
but many years before she had been the *wife* of *Menelaus*, the *Greek* king.
   1 1 1 1 1 1   1   1 1   1 1 1 1
Because this woman was very beautiful, the goddess *Venus* had given her to
Paris;   **13**
1 1   1 1 1   1   1 1 1   1   **10**
he had *judged Venus* to be the most *beautiful* of all the *goddesses*.
 1 1 1   1   1   1 1   1 1 1 1   **11**
'That night,' *said Deiphobus*, 'after we dragged the *wooden* horse into the *city*,
1 1   1   **3**
we *all* rejoiced.
 1   1 1   1   1   1   1 1 1 1 1 **11**
For we believed / thought the *Greeks* had gone away and the war was over.
   1   1   1   1   1   1   1 1
The *women* were *dancing* through the *city*, *and* among them *Helen*, holding a
 1   **9**
torch.'

Total: 120. Divide this total by 4 to reach final mark out of 30.   **[30]**

3
(a) telling (1) Aeneas (1) how (1) he had been killed (1)   **[4]**
(b) **(i)** the rest (1) believed (1) it was a light (1) for the dance(rs) (1) **[4]**
    (ii) a signal   (1) to the Greeks (1) who were waiting (1) in the ships (1)
       (for the signal) to attack (1) the city (1)   **[6]**
(c) he went (1) home (1) he did not know / to sleep (2)   **[4]**
(d) irony / sarcasm (or similar)   **[2]**
(e) removed (1) his arms (1) opened (1) the door (1) invited (1) Menelaus in (1) **[6]**
(f) Menelaus and friends (1) ran in (1)
   with swords (1) drawn (1)
   Deiphobus could not (1) resist long (1)
   he received (1) the wounds (1)

(Accept any three pairs.) [6]
(g) the wounds [2]
(h) (that the gods) punish (1) the Greeks (1) and above / before all (1)
Helen (1) in the same (1) way (1) [6]

[40 / 2 = 20]

Total for *Deiphobus* [60]

XII. *AESCULAPIUS COMES TO ROME*

1

(a) it was (1) killing (1) many (1) Romans (1) [4]
(b) they could (1) do (1) nothing (1) themselves (1) [4]
(c) to hear (1) the oracle (1) [2]
(d) don't come (1) to me (1) but (1) to my son (1) (Accept indirect speech.) [4]
(e) to seek (1) the home (1) of (1) Aesculapius / Apollo's son (1) [4]
(f) (they found out that) he lived (1) at Epidaurus (1) [2]

[20 / 2 = 10]

2

    1   1   1   1 11 1   **7**
The Romans, as soon as they learned that *Aeculapius* lived at *Epidaurus*,
1 1 1   1   1 1 1 1   **8**
sent a ship across the sea to that city / town.
1   1   1   1   1   **5**
In *the ship* were their ambassadors.
1   1   1   1   **4**
After / when the *ambassadors* (had) entered *Epidaurus*,
       1   1   1 1 1 1   1
they summoned *the town councillors* (and) begged them to give *the Romans*
1 11   **10**
their god,
   1   1   1 1 1   **6**
so that he could / might / to save the dying people.
1 1   1   1   1 1   1   1
Some *councillors* at once agreed, (but) others refused / did not want to hand
1   1   **10**
over *the god*.
1   1   11   1   **5**
They *argued* like this (through) all (the) day.
1 1 1   1 1   1   1   **7**
That night, while *all* were asleep,
     1   1 1 1 1   1   1 1   **8**
Aesculapius appeared to one of *the ambassadors* in *a dream*, holding *a sceptre*.

1 1 1   1   **4**
'Don't be afraid,' he said;
  1   1   1   1   1   1   1   1   1
'after leaving (behind) my *likeness* here, I myself shall gladly / willingly come
  1 1   **11**
with you.
  1 1 1   1   1 1   1 1   **8**
Look at this *serpent / snake*, which is round my *sceptre*;
  1   1 1 1 1 1 1 1 1   1   1
thus / this is how you will be able to know me: for I shall turn (myself) into
  1 1   **13**
such *a snake*,
  1   1 1 1 1   1 1   **7**
but I shall be bigger than this (one).'
  1   1   1   1 1   1 1
Having said / (after) saying these words *the god* left / the god said these words
and left.   **7**

Total: 120. Divide this total by 4 to reach final mark out of 30.   **[30]**

3
(a) at the temple (1) of the god (1) to seek (1) a sign (1) from (1) heaven / the
        sky (1)   **[6]**
(b) it was huge (1) its eyes (1) shone / gleamed (1) it appeared at once (1)   **[4]**
(c) he recognised (1) the god (1) he told (everyone) (1) to be silent (1)   **[4]**
(d) the citizens (1) and the Romans (1) worshipped (1) the god (1)   **[4]**
(e) to show (1) his approval (or similar) (1)   **[2]**
(f) it left (1) the temple (1) (it went) through (1) the middle (1) of the city (1)
        to the harbour (1) it set itself / went (1) on the ship (1)   **[8]**
(g) after (1) six days (1) at (1) dawn (1)   **[4]**
(h) **(i)** the whole (1) population (1) / all (1) the people (1) came (1) to the
                banks /river (1)   **[4]**
        (ii) he got rid of (1) the plague (1) without (1) delay (1)   **[4]**
                                                         [40 / 2 = 20]
                                    Total for *Aesculapius Comes to Rome* [60]

XIII. *THESEUS AND ARIADNE*

1
(a) king (1) of Crete (1)   **[2]**
(b) his son (1) was killed there (1)   **[2]**
(c) that seven girls (1) and young men (1) be sent (1) to Crete (1) for the
        Minotaur (1) to eat (1)   **[6]**

(d) son (1) of the king of Athens (1) [2]
(e) to go (1) himself (1) to kill (1) the Minotaur (1) and save (1) the rest (1) [6]
(f) he was afraid (1) he would be killed (1) [2]

[20 / 2 = 10]

2

    1 11   1   1   1 1 1   8
Theseus left *Athens* with the rest of the *Athenians*.
    1   1 1   1 1 1   1   1 1 1 1 1   1 1   14
When they reached the harbour of *Crete*, *Minos* the king led them to his *palace*.
    1   1   1   1   1   1 1   1 1
Before they were *led* into *the labyrinth*, where the *Minotaur* lived, they ate /
    1 1   11
had dinner.
      1   11   1   1 1 1   7
Next to Theseus sat *Ariadne*, the daughter of *Minos*.
    1   1 1   1 1   1 1   1   8
As soon as she saw / caught sight of the young man, she loved him.
      1   1   1   1 1   1   1 1   1 1 1   1   12
After_*dinner* therefore *Ariadne* came to_*Theseus*, bearing a sword and *wool*.
  1 1 11 1   1 1 1 1 1   1   1
Giving these to *Theseus*, she promised to come to the *labyrinth* the next day
  1 1 1 1   16
to free them.
    1   1 1   1 1   1   1   1   1   9
In the *labyrinth*, leaving the *rest* by the door, *Theseus threw* the *wool ahead*
    1 1   1   1 1   1 1   1 1   9
and followed it till he arrived at the *Minotaur* in the middle of the *labyrinth*.
    1   1   1   1   1 1   1 1   1 1   10
Although he had never before seen so dreadful a monster,
      1   1 1   1   4
he easily overcame it with the *sword*.
    1   1   1   1   1 1 1   1 1 1 1 1   12
When he had returned *to the others*, they waited till / for *Ariadne* to set them free.

Total: 120. Divide this total by 4 to reach final mark out of 30. [30]

3
(a) freed the Athenians (1) led them (1) from the palace (1) to the harbour (1) [4]
(b) after / it lasted (1) many hours (1) they reached / came to (1) Naxos (1) [4]
(c) it was (1) night (1) they were (1) tired (1) [4]
(d) drag (1) the ship (1) out of (1) the water (1) [4]
(e) next to (1) Theseus (1) [2]

(f) she was alone (1) she climbed (1) a hill (1) to look round (1) she saw (1) no one (1) [6]

(g) she was (1) very (1) sad (1) and very (1) angry (1) she had given him (1) her love (1) and help (1) [8]

(h) while she wondered (1) what to do (1) Bacchus saw her (1) and loved her (1) soon she forgot (1) Theseus (1) she married (1) Bacchus (1) [8]

[40 / 2 = 20]

Total for *Theseus and Ariadne* [60]

XIV. *ATTACK ON ROME*

1

(a) cruel [2]

(b) he was driven out (1) of Rome (1) [2]

(c) he was made / became (1) consul (1) [2]

(d) **(i)** a few (1) young men (1) wanted Tarquinius (1) to return (1) [4]

    (ii) they preferred (1) a king (1) to (1) a consul (1) [4]

(e) a slave (1) heard all (1) and reported (1) to Brutus (1) [4]

(f) his sons (1) were involved (1) [2]

[20 / 2 = 10]

2

  1   1 1 1   1   **5**

Now *Brutus* had / held a *trial*.

    1   1 1 1   1   **5**

Among the *defendants* were his two sons.

  1   1 1   1 1   1 1 1   1   1 1 1 1   1 **14**

Brutus, who *had* the greatest / very great power in the city, could save his *sons*;

1   1 1 1   1   **5**

but he did not free them.

1   1 1 1   1   1   1   1   1   1 **10**

For the people had given him *power*, because he was very *honest*.

1 1   1 1 1   1   1   1   1 **9**

He decided therefore that not his *sons but Rome* should / must be *saved*.

1   1 1   1 1 1   1 1 1   1 1   1 **12**

And so he ordered his guilty *sons* to be killed with the rest of the young men.

1   1   1   1   1 1 1 1 1   **9**

Now the citizens *gave Brutus* even greater honours.

1   1   1 1   1   1

Tarquinius, when he heard that the *conspiracy* had been / was found out,

1 1 1   **9**

was angry.

1   1 1   1   1   1   1 **7**

For he desired / wished to *have power* in_*Rome* again.

   1 1   1   1   1   1   **6**
It pleased him / he decided to attack the *city*.
  1   1   1   1 1   1 1   1 1   **9**
After / when he (had) persuaded other *cities* to *give* help,
     1   1   1   1 1   **5**
he hurried / marched to_*Rome* with a huge *army*.
  1   1   1 1   1   1   1   **7**
In the *battle* both the *son* of *Tarquinius and Brutus* were killed.
   1 1   1   1   1   1   1 1   **8**
The enemy having been led_away by *Tarquinius*, the *Romans* rejoiced.

Total: 120. Divide this total by 4 to reach final mark out of 30.   **[30]**

3
(a) Tarquinius tried (1) to capture Rome (1) with an even greater (1)
     army (1)   **[4]**
(b) it carried (1) the road (1) across the river (1) to the city (1)   **[4]**
(c) they were very (1) brave (1)
    they guarded (1) the bridge (1)
    night (1) and day (1)
    (Accept any two pairs.)   **[4]**
(d) that the enemy (1) would capture the bridge (1)   **[2]**
(e) the terrified (1) Romans (1) fled across the bridge (1) to the city (1)   **[4]**
(f) he was the leader (1) of the soldiers (1) guarding (1) the bridge (1)   **[4]**
(g) as soon as / when the last (1) men (1)
    crossed (1) the bridge (1)
    he ordered (1) his men (1)
    to destroy (1) the bridge (1)
    he stood (1) on the bridge (1)
    holding (1) a sword (1)
    one (1) against many (1)
    (Accept any five pairs.)   **[10]**
(h) he easily resisted (1) the enemy (1)
    when he heard (1) the shouts (1)
    of the men (1) destroying the bridge (1)
    he jumped (1) into the water (1)
    the city (1) was safe (1)
    (Accept any four pairs.)   **[8]**
                                             [40 / 2 = 20]
                                  Total for *Attack on Rome* [60]

XV. *THE ROPE*

1

(a) across / over (1) the sea (1)   [2]
(b) very (1) beautiful (1)   [2]
(c) he was the girl's (1) master (1) he was very (1) bad / evil (1)   [4]
(d) the young man had paid (1) a lot of money (1) but Labrax wanted (1) to sell her overseas (or similar) (1)   [4]
(e) the ship was driven (1) onto rocks (1) / was sinking (2)   [2]
(f) she leapt (1) into the sea (1) she reached (1) land (1) scarcely / barely (1) alive (1)   [6]

[20 / 2 = 10]

2

```
   1     1  11         1   1                                            6
```
Near the sea was the / a temple of *Venus*.
```
      1    1   1       1  1     1          1              1  1          9
```
By chance *Labrax* had promised he would / to bring / lead *Palaestra* to *the*
temple
```
1   1 1  1        1            1                                        6
```
to hand her over to the young man.
```
   1        1   1     1         1  1       1  1      1       1  1      13
```
This *young man* had wished / wanted to buy the slave-girl because he loved
```
   1    1                                                               
```
her greatly.
```
   1    1 1    1  1 1   1        1   1     1  1 1                       12
```
Now the girl was alone, and did not know what to do.
```
     1      1 1   1 1   1             1    1          1   1   1 1      12
```
There was a small house near *the temple*, in which / where an old man lived.
```
   1          1  1  1   1  1    1     1     1                           9
```
This *old man* had lost his daughter many years before:
```
1           1      1               1                1    1              6
```
for she had been captured *and* carried off / taken away by *robbers*.
```
1  1   1    1         1        1      1                                 7
```
He too was living / lived *alone now* with a few *slaves*.
```
   1     1         1                  1  1   1   1  1 11   1           11
```
The *girl*, having entered / after entering *the temple*, begged the priest to help her.
```
      1        1   1      1   1      1         1          1            
```
Meanwhile *Labrax*, who had *also* escaped from the ship, approached / came to
the *temple*.   8
```
   1          1         1     1  1  1               1                  7
```
Having caught sight of / seen the *girl*, he tried to *capture* / catch her.

<table>
<tr><td>1</td><td>1 1 1 1</td><td>1</td><td>1 1</td><td>8</td></tr>
</table>

1   1 1   1 1   1   1   1   **8**

The *old man*, (after) hearing shouts / cries in *the temple*, saved the *girl*;

     1   1   1 1 1   1   **6**

he ordered two *slaves* to hold *Labrax*.

Total: 120. Divide this total by 4 to reach final mark out of 30.   **[30]**

3

(a) **(i)**   standing (2) near (1) the temple (1)   [4]
      (ii)   the old man's (1) slave (1)   [2]
(b)   he was holding (1) a rope (1) by which he was dragging (1) a chest (1)
      along / across / over (1) the ground (1)   [6]
(c)   it had been on Labrax' (1) ship (1) it had fallen (1) in the sea (1)   [4]
(d)   she was very (1) happy (1) her toys (1) were inside it (1)   [4]
(e)   when (1) she was captured (1)
      she had them (1) with her (1)
      she used to play (1) with them (1)
      they would show (1) she was free-born (1)
      (Accept any three pairs.)   [6]
(f)   she described (1) them all (1) before Gripus (1) took them out (1)   [4]
(g)   he recognised (1) the toys (1) his daughter had had (1) similar / such
      (toys) (1) he realised / understood (2) that Palaestra (1) was his / that
      daughter (1)   [8]
(h)   everyone (1) was delighted / rejoiced (1)   [2]
                                                  [40 / 2 = 20]
                              Total for *The Rope* [60]

XVI. *AENEAS SEEKS A NEW HOME I*

1

(a)   captured (1) the city (1)   [2]
(b)   **(i)**   those not (1) killed (1)   [2]
      (ii)   in (1) the fields (1) near (1) the city (1)   [4]
(c)   children (2) old men (2)   [4]
(d)   they crossed (1) a mountain (1) at dawn (1) they came to the sea (1)   [4]
(e)   they were leaving (1) never (1) would they see (1) their native land
      again (1)   [4]
                                 [20 / 2 = 10]

2

     1   1   1 1   1   1   1   **7**

Aeneas and the Trojans sailed for many days.

   1   1   1   1 1   1 1   **7**

After they reached a small island,

1   1   1   1   1   1   1   1   1 1   1   1   1 1 1 1   **16**
where the temple of *Apollo* was, they begged the god to give them a new home.
1   1 1   1   1   1 1   1   1   **9**
Suddenly a voice was heard rising from the ground:
1   1   1 1   1   1   1   1   1   1   1   1   1   **13**
'You must return, *Trojans*, to that / the land in which you first lived.
1 1   1   1   1   1   1   1   1   1 1
Seek / look for (your) *ancient / former* mother: for here you will have great
1 1   **13**
power / empire.'
1   1   1   1 1   1   1   1   1   1   1   **11**
Rejoicing, *the Trojans* asked each other / among themselves where this *land* was.
1   1 1   1   1   1   1   1 1   1   1 1   **12**
Aeneas' father, now / already an old man, said, 'Listen, *Trojan* leaders,
1 1   1   1   1   1   1   **7**
and learn what / that which you can hope (for).
1   1   1   1   1   1 1   1   1 1
In the middle of the sea lies the island of *Crete, where* stands a second /
1   1   **12**
another Mount *Ida*.
1   1   1   1   1   1   1
Our *first father, Teucer,* sailed *from there* to *Asia*, to establish *the Trojan*
1   **8**
kingdom.
1   1   1   1   1   **5**
We must therefore make for / seek *Crete*.'

Total: 120. Divide this total by 4 to reach final mark out of 30.   **[30]**

3
(a)   three (1) days (1)   [2]
(b) (i)   began (1) to build (1) city (1) walls (1)   [4]
         (ii)   *statim* (2) *brevi tempore* (2)   [4]
         (iii)   houses (1) complete (1) forum (1) incomplete (1) temples (1)
incomplete (1)   [6]
(c)   it attacked (1) men (1) and corn (1) very many / most (1) Trojans (1) died (1)   [6]
(d) (i)   in the middle (1) of the night (1) a god appeared (1) in a dream (1)
standing (1) in the moonlight (1)   [6]
         (ii)   it was sent (1) by the gods (1)   [2]
(e)   he had led (1) the Trojans (1) to Crete (1) not to Italy (1)   [4]
(f)   he reported / announced (1) the dream (1) to the rest (1) next day (1) they
left (1) in tears (1)   [6]
                                                              [40 / 2 = 20]
                              Total for *Aeneas Seeks a New Home I* [60]

XVII. *AENEAS SEEKS A NEW HOME II*

1

(a) leading the Trojans (1) across / over the sea (1) [2]
(b) a new home (1) in Italy (1) [2]
(c) she hated them (1) she did not want them (1) to reach (1) Italy (1) [4]
(d) she raised / there was (1) a storm (1) the ships were driven / carried (1) to Africa (1) [4]
(e) almost (1) worn out (1) [2]
(f) climbed (1) a hill (1) to spy out / inspect / look at (1) the place (1) [4]
(g) she appeared as / took the form of (1) a girl (1) [2]

[20 / 2 = 10]

2

<pre>
 1   1   1 11 1   1   1   1 1   1   11
</pre>
Venus said, 'This land is *Carthage*, whose queen *is Dido*.
<pre>
      1   1   1   1   1   1 1   7
</pre>
Dido will receive / welcome / accept you gladly / willingly in(to) her city.
<pre>
  1   1 1 1   1   1 1   1   1 1 1 1 1   13
</pre>
For the *queen* does not have / has no husband, because (her) brother killed him.
<pre>
 1   1   1   1   4
</pre>
She fears (her) *brother* greatly / very much.
<pre>
  1   1 1   1   1   1 1 1   1   1   1   11
</pre>
Then the goddess asked *Aeneas* who he was *and* from_where he had come.
<pre>
     1 1   1 1 1   1   6
</pre>
Aeneas replied that he was (a) *Trojan*.
<pre>
  1 1   1 1   1 1   1 1   1   1   1   11
</pre>
'The gods,' *he said*, 'do not favour us.' 'But I *favour* you,' the *goddess* said.
<pre>
  1   1   1 1 1   1   1   1   8
</pre>
Having spoken / when she had spoken these words, she at once went away.
<pre>
     1   1   1   1 1   1 1 1 1   1   10
</pre>
Aeneas, who now *recognised* his mother, followed her with his voice:
<pre>
  1 1 1 1   1   1   1   1   1 1   1   10
</pre>
'You are too cruel, *mother*. Why do you deceive me like_this?
<pre>
      1 1 1   1   1   5
</pre>
Why don't you give me (your) right hand?'
<pre>
  1   1 1   1   1   1   6
</pre>
When *Aeneas* (had) returned sad(ly) to his men / people,
<pre>
  1   1   1   1   1   5
</pre>
he announced / reported / related / told them what had happened.
<pre>
  1   1 1 1
</pre>
The(ir) ships left / after leaving their ships / when they had left their ships

96

1	1					6

near the sea,

1	1	1	1 1		1	1	7

they set out to seek / look for / make for *Dido*'s *city*.

Total: 120. Divide this total by 4 to reach final mark out of 30. [30]

3

(a) cross (1) a mountain (1) [2]
(b) it was so (1) big (1) and (1) beautiful (1) that (1) they admired it (1) [6]
(c) in all parts (1) of the city (1) there was a multitude (1) of men (1) they
were working (1) carefully / hard (1) [6]
(d) walls (2) streets / roads (2) forum   (2) [6]
(e) (i) temple (1) of Juno (1) [2]
(ii) it was very (1) big (1) / the biggest (2) [2]
(f) he left (1) the rest (1) outside (1) the city (1) [4]
(g) (i) the Trojan (1) War (1) [2]
(ii) (he saw) (so) many (1) comrades / companions / friends (1)
fighting (1) bravely (1) (who were) now (1) dead (1) [6]
(h) he believed (1) the queen (1) would help (1) him / give him help (1) [4]
|40 / 2 = 20|

Total for *Aeneas Seeks a New Home II* |60|

XVIII. *PIRATES I*

1

(a) to be (1) a priest (1) [2]
(b) in Rome (1) he held (1) the greatest / very great (1) power (1) [4]
(c) if you make me (1) a priest (1) I shall be (1) grateful (to you) (1) [4]
(d) he believed (1) Caesar (1) was too (1) young (1) [4]
(e) he had it (1) in mind (1) to kill (1) him (1) [4]
(f) he fled (1) from Rome (1) [2]
|20 / 2 = 10|

2

1	1		1	1		1				5

Caesar was escaping from the city.

1	1	1		1 1	11	1 1	11	1		12

He was sailing across the sea with a few friends in a small ship / boat.

1 1	1	1	1	1	1 1 1 1 1	1 1 1	1 1			16

Some *pirates*, of whom there were many at that time in all parts of the *sea*,

1	1	1 1	1	1 1	1	1	1	1	1 1	14

captured and took / led them to a small island; here they held *Caesar* prisoner
/ captive.

```
1           1              1 1  1              1     1              1   8
```
When they sought / asked for a price of *twenty talents* for his life, *Caesar* laughed.
```
      1    1      1    1    1       1      1              7
```
He shouted they did not know whom they had captured.
```
1       1   1  1 1                    1              6
```
He promised to give / that he would give them *fifty talents*.
```
   1    1       1   1  1  1      1              8
```
He sent his *friends* to *Rome* to look for this money.
```
 1      1        1      1   1   1   1   1       1  1  1  1
```
While he was waiting for them, he tried to order the *pirates* to do what
```
       1     1                                        14
```
he_himself wanted.
```
    1      1  1 1              1     1     1      1       8
```
He even *recited* poems / songs *and speeches* which he had written,
```
 1      1             1       1    1    1  1 1       8
```
and unless / if (not) they *applaud*ed, he *call*ed them very stupid / foolish.
```
   1       1       1      1    1   1   1    1      1    1    1
```
When he often shouted that he would kill them, they believed these words
```
1 1    1                                              14
```
were *empty*.

Total: 120. Divide this total by 4 to reach final mark out of 30. [30]

3
(a) his friends (1) returned (1) bringing (1) the money / price (1) [4]
(b) to return (1) to the island (1) on which he had been (1) a captive (1) [4]
(c) he attacked (1) them (1) he captured (them) (1) easily (1) [4]
(d) he recovered (1) the fifty (1) talents (1) which he had given (1) to the
    pirates (1) he seized (1) everything (1) which they had (1) [8]
(e) they were taken (1) to the nearest (1) city (1) to prison (1) [4]
(f) **(i)** he asked (1) the governor (to punish them) (1) [2]
    (ii) he realised / understood (1) that the governor (1) wanted (1)
    money (1) not (1) men (1) [6]
(g) the governor (1) sending soldiers (1) to seize (1) the money (1) [4]
(h) he dragged them out (1) and killed them (1) he was richer (1)
    than before (1) [4]

[40 / 2 = 20]
Total for *Pirates I* [60]

XIX. *PIRATES II*

1
(a) in all (1) parts (1) / every (1) part (1) of (1) the sea (1) [4]
(b) the Roman legions (1) were fighting (1) against (1) other enemies (1) [4]

(c) they attacked (1) ships (1) islands (1) cities (1) [4]
(d) they became very (1) rich (1) [2]
(e) they thought (1) there was (great) honour (in such a life) (1) [2]
(f) they had many (1) harbours (1) their ships were (1) (very) fast (1) [4]

[20 / 2 = 10]

2

1 1 1 1 1 1 1 1 1 1 1 1
The worst *crime* of the pirates was to seize / carry off *public officials or* rich
1 1 **14**
citizens,
1 1 1 1 1 1 1 **7**
then to demand money / a ransom for them.
1 1 1 1 1 1 1 1 1 1 1 1 1 **13**
Those captives who shouted / claimed that they were *Roman* citizens were killed,
1 1 1 1 1 1 1 1 1 1
unless they promised that their men / people would give the *pirates* very
1 1 **12**
much *money*.
1 11 1 1 1 1 1 1 1 1 1 1 **13**
Soon the sea was so full of *pirates* that no one wished to sail;
1 1 1 1 1 1 11 **8**
the people at / of *Rome* therefore did not receive corn.
1 1 1 1 1 1 1 1 1 **9**
At last the senators / senate sent out *Pompey* to crush the *pirates*;
1 1 1 1 1 1 1 1 1 **9**
power by / over land and sea was given to him.
1 1 11 1 1 1 **7**
He also *received five hundred* ships *and twenty*-four legions.
1 1 1 1 1 1 1 **7**
Pompey set out from *Rome* with all these *forces*.
1 1 1 1 **4**
Having *divided* the *sea* into *thirteen* parts,
1 1 1 1 1 1 1 **7**
the *Roman* leaders attacked the *pirates* in *all* the *parts simultaneously*;
1 1 1 1 1 **5**
in this way they were *surrounded and* captured.
11 1 1 1 **5**
Soon the whole *sea* was *free*.

Total: 120. Divide this total by 4 to reach final mark out of 30. [30]

3
(a) he returned (1) to Rome (1) [2]

(b) very many / most (1) citizens (1) met / came together (1) to the gates (1)
to greet him (1) as he entered the city (1) [6]

(c) the shops (1) were full (1) of all (1) things (1) [4]

(d) a few (1) pirates (1) who had not been (1) killed (1) escaped (1) there / to
Cilicia (1) where they had (1) a camp (1) [8]

(e) he feared (1) that the pirates (1) would (try to) attack (1) sailors /
travellers (1) [4]

(f) (*tam*) *celeriter* (2) (so) quickly (2) *brevissimo* (1) *tempore* (1) in a very
short (1) time (1) [8]

(g) the worst (1) were imprisoned (1) the rest (1) were freed (1) their camp
(1) was destroyed (1) [6]

(h) it lasted / was over in (1) three months (1) [2]

[40 / 2 = 20]

Total for *Pirates II* [60]

XX. *CIPUS*

1

(a) (he was) a Roman (1) general (*not* emperor) (1) [2]

(b) he had defeated (1) the enemy (1) near (1) the / a river (1) [4]

(c) catch sight of himself (1) in the river (1) [2]

(d) he saw (1) horns (1) on (top of) (1) his head (1) [4]

(e) because he did not (1) believe (1) the sign (1) was true / real (1) [4]

(f) that the sign should be (1) a happy one (1) for him (1) and the Roman
people (1) [4]

[20 / 2 = 10]

2

    1 1   1 1   1   1   1   1   1   9

Cipus placed / set up an altar to the gods near the city of *Rome*.

   1   1   1   1   1   6

There he poured wine and killed *the victims*.

  1   1 1   1   1   11 11 1   1   1   12

When the priest inspected *the entrails* / insides, he saw signs of great things.

  1   1 1   11 1   1   1   1   1

Then, (after) raising / having lifted his eyes to the horns on *Cipus'* head, he

  1   1   1   13

said, 'Hello, king.

  1 1   1   11 1   1   1 1   1   1   1   12

For all the citizens of this place will obey you *and* your *horns* willingly / gladly.

  1   11   1   1   5

Now hurry back into *the city*.

  1   1   1   1   1 1

For having been accepted / received / if you are received into the *city*, you will

1   7

1
be *king.*'

1   1   1 1 1 1   1 1 1   1   1
Cipus, however, terrified by these words, refused / did not want to approach
1   12
the *city.*

1   1 1 1   1   1   6
He begged the *gods* not to *permit* such things / a thing:
1 1 1 1 1 1   1   1 1 1   9
for he preferred to go into *exile* than to be *king,*
1   1 1 1   1   1   1   1   1 1 1 11
because, like most / very many *Romans*, he thought / believed all *kings* to be bad.
1   1   1   1 1   1 1   1
At once (after) calling together the people *and* senators / senate *outside* the
1   9
walls *of Rome,*
1 1   1   1 1   1 1   1
and hiding his *horns* / with his horns hidden, he tried to avert / turn away such
1   9
a bad *thing.*

Total: 120. Divide this total by 4 to reach final mark out of 30.   **[30]**

3

(a) someone (1) is present / here (1) if you don't (1) drive him out (1) he will
be (1) king (1) (Accept indirect speech.)   **[6]**

(b) he wears / has horns (1) on his head (1)   **[2]**

(c) (a priest said that) if he entered (1) Rome (1) he would be (1) king (1)
this is the same (1) as line 1 (or similar) (1)   **[6]**

(d) (i) the gates (1) were open (1)   **[2]**
     (ii) Cipus (1) stopped him (1)   **[2]**

(e) he was hiding (1) his horns (1) he was pretending to talk (1) about
someone else (1) he was trying (1) to persuade (1) the Romans (1) not to
let him in (1) (There is scope here for alternative answers: use
judgement.)   **[8]**

(f) they wanted (1) to know (1) who (1) the man was (1) they inspected (1)
heads (1)   **[6]**

(g) they looked at (1) his head (1) / they understood (1) the matter (1)   **[2]**

(h) they gave him (1) a large (1) farm (1) near the city (1) because they did
not dare (1) admit him (1)   **[6]**

[40 / 2 = 20]

Total for *Cipus* [60]